ZODIAC

Co Londonderry

Edited by Steve T

First published in Great Britain in 2002 by
YOUNG WRITERS
Remus House,
Coltsfoot Drive,
Peterborough, PE2 9JX
Telephone (01733) 890066

HB ISBN 0 75433 506 2
SB ISBN 0 75433 507 0

FOREWORD

Young Writers was established in 1991 with the aim of promoting creative writing in children, to make reading and writing poetry fun.

Once again, this year proved to be a tremendous success with over 41,000 entries received nationwide.

The Zodiac competition has shown us the high standard of work and effort that children are capable of today. The competition has given us a vivid insight into the thoughts and experiences of today's younger generation. It is a reflection of the enthusiasm and creativity that teachers have injected into their pupils, and it shines clearly within this anthology.

The task of selecting poems was a difficult one, but nevertheless, an enjoyable experience. We hope you are as pleased with the final selection in *Zodiac Co Londonderry* as we are.

CONTENTS

Fiona Hill	70
Amy Watton	71
Emma Collins	72
Elizabeth Crowe	72
Carli Connor	73
Alison Archer	73
Sharon Hoy	74
Lesley-Anne Peters	74
Rachael Vauls	75
Alison Cameron	76
Naomi Moore	77
Victoria Harbinson	78

Limegrove School

Christena Moore	78
William O'Hara	79
Scott McElwee	79
Shona McCloskey	80
Matthew Crawford	80

Magherafelt High School

Ryan Johnston	81
Leanne Nesbitt	81
Philip Crossett	82
Alan Jones	82
Christopher Morrow	83
June Speers	84
William Davison	84
Andie Purvis	85
Charlene Gilmore	86
Emma Charlene Campbell	87
Andrew Stewart	88
Kelly McKee	88
Michael Hutchinson	89
Aaron Purvis	90
Richard Davis	90
Sam Lee	91
Andrea Henderson	92

William Brown	92
Claire Moore	93
Hanna Lawrence	93
Lisa Bowman	94
Claire Wallace	94
Gyles McAllen	95
Ruth Linton	96
James Dempsey	96
Claire Fullerton	97
Sharon Montgomery	97
Laura Brown	98
Gareth Booth	98
Lee-Anne Duncan	99
Matthew Gallick	99
Cathy Gilmour	100
Emma Palmer	100
Ian Brown	101
Robert Glendinning	102
James Higgins	102
Pamela Davis	103
Nicola Jordan	103
Emma Forde	104
Zara Morrison	104
Sharon Ferguson	105
Leanne Davison	106
Samantha Finlay	106
Laura Jamison	107
Stacey Hassan	108
Julie Gregg	108
David Barfoot	109
Stacey Boone	110
William Henderson	110
Thomas Shannon	111
Matthew Hyndman	111
Andrew Derby	112
Gary Jordan	112
Alan McClean	113
Paul Somerville	113

The Poems

SIMPLY THE BEST

In Belfast Town a lad was born,
His name was Georgie Best.
He could play from dawn to dusk,
And take on any test.

In Manchester he went to play,
For United's famous Reds.
Bobby, Denis, Brian and George,
The greatest, Busby's ever led.

European glory was in their sights,
Only Benfica stood in their way.
Georgie's magic won the match,
Celebrating started that day.

It seemed those days would never end,
But Georgie had to rest.
Alcohol took those glory days,
But he's still better than the rest.

Now he's home in County Down,
Ballyhalbert is the place.
The greatest genius of his time,
Even though he fell from grace.

Neal Linnegan (12)
Coleraine Academical Institution

THE HAUNTED HOUSE

Up the stairs I went,
The doors suddenly opened.
A voice said, 'Come in!'

Mark Boyd (12)
Coleraine Academical Institution

POETIC HEADACHES

What should my title be?
How can I start?
I should put this page up on a wall,
And hit it with a dart!

Stray thoughts are flying through my head,
I think I should just go to bed,
I just can't think of something new,
I need ideas *now*, out of the blue.

Perhaps 'Nature At Its Finest,'
No, that's been used before,
Or what about a 'Monstrous Nightmare,'
No, I need a little more.

This homework is impossible!
My pen won't write a thing,
I think I'll just forget it,
And put it in the bin.

But then I will be punished,
I haven't done my work!
Maybe I could fake an illness?
Or pretend I've gone berserk!

Why can't I write a poem,
A clever piece of writing?
My mind just keeps on spilling words,
But they're really not exciting.

The thought of lines has made me sick,
It's forced me into action,
I've written this lot, double quick,
Wow! Poetry's really *smashin'*!

Mark Laverty (12)
Coleraine Academical Institution

MUHAMMAD ALI (CASSIUS CLAY)

Young Cassius Clay had a treasured possession,
That pride and joy was a brand new bike.
But one fine day that bike was stolen,
And from here on he learned to fight.

At the '60 Olympics Clay won gold,
The start of his run to become the best.
He claimed he was better than Floyd Patterson,
Saying 'Some day I'll whup you and all the rest!'

He said, 'I am The Greatest, I'm Muhammad Ali,'
When he beat Sonny Liston 'The Bear'.
His title was stolen over Vietnam,
Because he said it was wrong to fight there.

Ali returned to the ring once again,
Everyone thought he'd get beat.
'I'm still The Greatest!' he laughed at them all,
'I'll never accept a defeat.'

The fiercest of rivals was 'Smokin' Joe Frazier.'
They fought three times in the ring.
The 'Thrilla In Manila' was the best of the fights,
And when Joe was beaten The Greatest was King.

So this is the story of Muhammad Ali,
Better than all the rest.
Sadly struck down with Parkinson's Syndrome,
But still 'The Greatest.'

Philip Taylor (12)
Coleraine Academical Institution

MY FIRST DAY

It's my first day at Inst.
I jump out of bed
I put on my uniform
And get myself fed.
I'm feeling quite nervous
But I'm also excited
The school's huge
But I've new friends
And so I'm delighted.
The teachers are nice
And so are the dinners
It's better than primary school
I'm on to a winner!

Lots of subjects on my timetable
And lots of books to carry
I hope I'm not bullied
And have no need to worry
I'm a first former now
And I like my new school
I want to do seven years
That would be really cool!

Adam Goudy (11)
Coleraine Academical Institution

AT NIGHT

Bats flapping loudly
Banshees wailing quietly
Swiftly ghosts appear.

Michael Topping (11)
Coleraine Academical Institution

TRUST ME

'Trust me,'
The two words, which make my skin turn inside out and itch all over.

You can't trust many,
All people care about is money and themselves.

The world is full of deceitfulness,
How can the words 'Trust me' mean anything?

Maybe I'm being a bit harsh,
But this place we call Earth isn't as good as it's made out to be.

'Trust me,'
The two words which flip my head into an eternal abyss.

Let this poem win,
'Trust me!' I'll be grateful.

You see the words mean nothing,
Trust is little, especially where money is.

'Trust me,'
Sometimes I wonder if I can trust myself.

Chris McAteer (13)
Coleraine Academical Institution

HALLOWE'EN NIGHT

Ghosts and ghouls are out
To suck the fun out of here
Until morning comes.

Eric Stewart-Moore
Coleraine Academical Institution

THE BATTLE ON CHRISTMAS DAY

Silence.
No artillery, no shots break through the still air.
Only the crunching of foot on snow.
'Don't shoot,' said the voice.
'Don't shoot.'
A short man breaks through the mist rising from the mud and snow.
He holds no gun, only a bottle of brandy.
'I brought a gift,' he says holding out the bottle.
'It's Christmas, after all.'

The day went on.
More gifts were passed. Rivals drank together with glee.
The party boomed, rations were shared,
They ate quite merrily.
Then night came. The visitors went back,
Happy in their brief friendship.
The morning awoke with the sounds of the artillery's dawn symphony.
Machine guns rattled,
Bullets whizzing to and fro.

David Anderson
Coleraine Academical Institution

SPOOKED

When do you get spooked?
When you watch a scary film
Or walk in the dark?

Andrew McGrath (11)
Coleraine Academical Institution

MY FIRST DAY

Oh no, I feel sick,
The summer holidays went too quick!
There's too many things going on in my head,
Why can't I just stay in bed!
The teachers, the homework and making new friends,
So much pressure, the trouble never ends.

I arrived at the bus stop at ten to eight,
Surprise, surprise, the bus has come late!
We arrived at the school, *big, scary and old!*
There are ghosts in the building or so I'm told.
I always got lost, so the prefects would say,
'Turn left, turn right' but it was never the way.
When I got to the classroom the teachers weren't bad,
And I made some friends I never had!
On the way home I missed the bus,
Then I realised Inst. isn't such a big fuss!

Casey McKinney (11)
Coleraine Academical Institution

AUTUMN

As I slowly walk through the park
I wonder about the noises I can hear,
Like the birds singing, the trees swaying,
And the leaves crunching beneath my feet.

> The different colours of autumn are fascinating,
> And can resemble so much.
> I see different patterns
> And the different pictures that nature provides.

Carol Haslett (14)
Coleraine High School

PARADISE

Is there a place in the world
Where no tragedies occur?
Where the sky is a shade of blue
Like you've never seen before.

Where there is no such thing as fear
Only laughter and singing and smiles everywhere
There's no such thing as racism or crime
I've heard of this place before
But don't know if it exists.

It's hard to believe a place can be this perfect
I want to find this amazing place
This paradise, this wonderful dream.

Where the sky is the most amazing blue
With its sandy beaches and the green sea
No crime, only happiness
I'm going to find this paradise. My dream.

Clare Willis (12)
Coleraine High School

A PENCIL SHARPENER

It squeaks, it turns, it grinds,
I twist, I turn, I fight,
But there is no escape
From this dark murderer.

Its sharp blade digs in,
It turns around and around
It's taking off my skin
Ah, that really hurt!

I can see my skin falling off
It's all bent and twisted
And my head is now a lot shorter
As I try to go back to work.

My body shakes like mad and
I can feel it wobbling,
Oh no not again
It's back to the torturing for me!

Leanne Black (12)
Coleraine High School

THE WHITE CHRISTMAS

I got out of bed
I shivered, oh it's so cold.
I peeped through the curtains
Now I know why!
Everywhere was covered in a blanket of snow
It was the first white Christmas since 1996.

I jumped for joy
I thought of making snowmen and snowballs
I ran downstairs shouting on my way
Watch out or I'll give you a fright
Deep inside I was so excited.

I grabbed my coat, woolly hat and gloves
I pushed my feet into my tiny boots
Made a dash to the door
Everything was white as white can be
Every fence and every tree
Across the field I go
Leaving footprints in the snow.

Kathryn Taylor (12)
Coleraine High School

AUTUMN LEAVES

The leaves make an entrance,
And flutter down from the tree.
Slowly and silently they flutter, like dancers.

One by one, they dance through the air,
Each one a different colour from the next.

The world is their stage,
As they glide gracefully around me.

The soft whistle of the breeze,
Is the music that they dance to
All through the day, they dance.

When they reach the ground,
Their solo is over,
And another dancer glides through the air,
Performing to its audience.

When the day comes to an end,
So does their show, but they put on another performance
Again tomorrow
I know I will be there to see it.

Kirsty McCandless (14)
Coleraine High School

SELFISH PEOPLE

We have our clothes, we have our food
And clean, safe drinking water.
We should stop and think the pain and suffering
Of what they're going through.

We forget and take for granted
What we already have
We waste, we abuse, we shout and we use
Can we stop and think what we can do?

The damage has been done but it's not too late
To save the world from wrong
We should open our eyes and see
That there are more people in the world than you.

Roxanna Dehaghani (12)
Coleraine High School

THE WIND

The sound when you're lying in your bed
When your throat tightens,
You hide under your covers
And wish it was morning.

It sounds like ghosts and ghouls
And feels like them too,
Its best friend is the rain
They work together to scare me out of my bed.

The way it flies around you
Outside, first thing in the morning,
It freezes your fingers and toes
Oh, I hate wind.

But I suppose . . .
What would we do without it,
On those blistering hot days
We need that lovely cool breeze.

The way it blows your hair,
On a hot summer's day,
Or the way it curls around you
And makes all the trees sway.

So where would we be without it?

Louise Caldwell (12)
Coleraine High School

NO ONE CAN DO ANYTHING

The noises all around this place
The smell of new hot fire
And no one can do anything.

The sights of smoke, grey and black
Like lambs wool burning up
And no one can do anything.

The screams of people calling out
For rescue from this terror
And no one can do anything.

The debris falling from the sky
Like rain hard and cold
And no one can do anything.

The people running far and wide
Trying to escape this thing
And no one can do anything.

The people watching, waiting, scared,
Praying for one inside,
What can they do, but pray?

Lynsey Workman (12)
Coleraine High School

HELL AND HEAVEN

What happens after death?
Some people say it's just another day,
And you lie in your coffin forever,
But my thoughts are very different.

You either go to Hell or Heaven,
Hell is bad like nobody knows,
Hell is fire, that always glows,
An eternal *nightmare*!

Heaven is as Heaven does
A paradise that lasts forever,
No sad fears or no tears,
Living my life with the angels.

Lauren Watson (12)
Coleraine High School

ALL A DREAM

In the clouds I'm floating around
    Up and down the angels sound
My big white wings are flapping about
    I dance, fly, scream and shout.

What's this I see coming down the lane?
    Oohh my word, it is a golden train,
But there's no hurry for a seat,
    They're all walking calmly, no scurrying feet.

There's no first class or business,
    Everyone's the same.
Everyone is peaceful,
    On this golden train.

Now the light is starting to fade
    And all the sweet angels too.
Where has all the silk and satin gone
    And the white fluffy wings I once had on?

It was all a sweet, sweet dream
    No more pleasure anywhere to be seen
No more golden trains
    Just a lot of fuss and hassle and no lanes.

Zoë Houston (12)
Coleraine High School

FAME

For my whole life I've wished to have fame,
Whatever the cost I'm willing, I'm game,
But what I shall be I really can't guess,
Whatever it is, I shall try my best.

Perhaps a magician and pull rabbits out of hats,
Or a world class vet curing puppies and cats,
I could be a rock star like Elvis - The King,
Maybe a boxer and fight in the ring.

I could be a presenter to entertain the world,
Or a model with a short skirt and my hair in curls,
A mad scientist to make things blow up,
I could be a jockey and win a shiny cup.

A movie star makes loads of money,
Or a comedian (I can be really funny),
Maybe a footballer and score a few goals,
A golfer to put the ball in the hole.

A wonderful doctor could be my aim,
Or I could break a world record - that would bring some fame!
I might be an astronaut and shoot into space,
A very speedy sprinter, I could win a race.

There are so many things I could choose,
But there's no matter if I lose,
Out of all the things I could be,
I will always be *me*!

Ashleigh Kilgore (13)
Coleraine High School

THE VIOLINIST

An empty hall,
With nothing but chairs
A stage is just waiting
For someone to appear and break the silence.

As time goes by
Moods start to change.

People rushing in and out
Get ready for the performance.
The audience file into their seats and wait in anticipation,
Everything is silent.

He stands on stage
With great posture and pose
And lifts up his instrument,
At last the silence is broken.

He addresses his fiddle
Bow perfectly rosined and square to the string,
He pulls a note.

With grace and ease he glides the bow
Like skaters spinning on a frozen pond.
Lost in time.

He holds the audience captive,
All prisoners to music
Until the end.

Krystina Kyle (14)
Coleraine High School

I HATE WAITING

Oh I hate waiting!
It curls around me like a slimy snake then
Hits me like a ton of bricks,
Then I'm chaos to live with,
I prance up and down the room like a big elephant,
And shout and scream and bang my feet,
I sometimes even talk to myself.
Oh I hate it, I hate it, I hate it,
My mum doesn't seem to understand,
She just says, 'You've got to wait your turn dear!'
Huh 'Wait dear, wait, dear, wait dear.' That's all I ever hear.
Oh I hate that word so much
It sends a shiver down my back every time I say it
Please don't make me wait again.

Kathryn Johnston (12)
Coleraine High School

CHILLS WITH THRILLS

The stimulating snow hills,
With their dark white, glinting eyes,
Look at me with a welcoming sense of adventure.
The sky's shady blue, the wind's ripping chill,
Invite me to join with them in
A new adventurous game.
The smell of the whirling snow around me,
With its cruel, assertive touch.
Sweeps me through the mountains,
On its icy, unflinching back.

Sandra Kennedy (14)
Coleraine High School

CARNAGE

On a glorious September morning,
When America had just came alive.
Out of the air with no warning,
An unexpected guest did arrive.

There was smoke and flames galore,
And people all stood in despair.
The buildings that they had seen before,
Were now beyond repair.

Firemen and police came to the scene,
When all they heard were the screams.
People alive under the rubble,
What a sad day with so much trouble.

With somebody's loved ones still not found,
Everything now has burnt to the ground.
The search does go on and the hope is still there,
But everyone's lives feel so bare.

Zorrina Harbinson (12)
Coleraine High School

I WISH

I wish for happiness,
In this world of hurt.
I wish for love,
To keep me warm in life.
I wish for peace,
In this land of hate.
I wish for health,
To keep me fresh and elated.
I wish to be free from this horrible place of cruelty.

Stacey Kennedy (12)
Coleraine High School

SWEETS

Sweets I love them,
Love them I do.
They're sweet and sour,
And nice to chew.

There's chocolate and toffee,
And strawberries and fudge.
Umm I love them,
I love them so much.

Crisps are OK,
Nuts are yuck.
But lollipops,
Are nice to suck.

Chewing gum,
All flavours and types.
Some chew it and spit it out,
Others stick it on the bedposts over night.

Ice cream,
It comes in tubs and cones,
But it's the real Italian I like,
When I get home.

Robyn Friel (12)
Coleraine High School

THE WIND

He comes,
He goes.

Darting and dashing,
No one can catch him.

Whizzing and whirling,
He sends people swirling.

He leaves a trail of destruction
To show where he's been.

He has so much power,
But can never be seen.

He is mysterious
He is the wind.

Gillian Kane (14)
Coleraine High School

HATRED

It is a feeling that overcomes me
When someone says nasty things
To me!

It is a feeling that overcomes me
When I hear a song that I really
Hate the sound of!

It is a feeling that overcomes me
When bigoted people fight over
Whose religion is better!

It is a feeling that overcomes me
When I watch the news and see
Terrorist attacks!

It is a feeling that overcomes me
Every day of my life and sooner
Or later it will all come out!

Nikki McCahon (13)
Coleraine High School

THE FOOTBALL

Instead of being up high,
The moon is at my feet.
It doesn't shine at all
It's quite small.
Everyone is running to see it
I pick it up in my hands,
I kick, kick high
But it comes back down.
Someone's running and kicking the moon
It hits a net
People cheer and celebrate at the sight,
A whistle blows,
A man picks up the moon,
He carries it away.

Emma Harkness (12)
Coleraine High School

THE POOR STREET

People and vehicles causing an uproar,
Shopkeepers shouting at bystanders.
Shops like shacks, colourful yet dull,
Vehicles rusty and frail.
Broken power lines and cracked cobbles
Give a bad appearance to the street.
Torn clothes and tired faces,
Show a poor society.
Fumes and cigarette smoke,
Cause a smell round every corner?

Hilary Andrews (14)
Coleraine High School

TRANQUILLITY

As I sail along I think of the calm,
Tranquil place before me,
Full of beauty and splendour,
The wind stirring gently through the trees,
The song of the birds,
The gentle flow of water,
All the colours of the beautiful trees merge into one,
Exquisite emerald,
I touch the water to ensure I am not dreaming,
It is true, I am really here,
I smell the flowers in the air,
The freshness of the woods,
How could such a place exist?
So little here, yet so much to see,
In this oasis of tranquillity.

Joelene Campbell (14)
Coleraine High School

A DOG'S HEAD

Woof! Can I have some more water?
Make sure it's cold or I won't drink it.
I fetched you a stick, now throw it away,
So I can get it and we can play.
Where's my squeaky bone gone to?
Doesn't matter, I'll just chew this shoe.
Take me for a walk in the park
I want to chase Tiddles and ducks in the lake.
But I'm not getting wet like I do,
When I take a bath, wooo! (howl).
Get me a blanket for my house,
It gets cold and draughty at night.

Charlene McCubbin (14)
Coleraine High School

LIQUORICE, MY CAT

Liquorice is my cat,
She is all black,
With green eyes,
She is very small.

She is pathetic!
She can't jump onto the window sill,
Not even a picnic table
She can just about jump onto a chair.

Liquorice needs a ramp to get in the cat flap,
She has to be lifted onto the window sill,
When she is on the window sill she takes forever to get down,
When you walk into the kitchen at night all you see is her eyes.

Liquorice has a play friend,
The cat behind us,
They play fight, but he hurts her sometimes,
He is always like the speed of light when he sees you watching.

Liquorice does not even leave her own garden,
I have come to one reason why she does not jump,
She is cross-eyed!
I still have to find out the others.

Stephanie Brooks (12)
Coleraine High School

THE CAT'S HEAD

Full of wisdom and cunning,
Dreams of chasing and running,
Pouncing and catching a mouse,
Leaving it by the door of the house.

Clean and tidy is the way they like it
Sleeping on your lap while you sit
Thinking of food!
They'd eat it all if they only could.

Fiona Thornton (13)
Coleraine High School

ZERO-G

Gravity is awesome power,
And tender manipulation.
It holds distant stars and galaxies together.
It makes a pin drop.

Without gravity:

Rain would follow the wind,
Flitting and flowing like tiny butterflies
In a meadow.

My hair would writhe and twist,
Like snakes on the head
Of Medusa.

My food would curl and squirm,
And dance above my spinning plate
And floating chair.

It would be
An up-less, down-less, north-less, south-less,
Swirling, twirling, whirling, winding,
Weaving, looping, churning,
Muddled kind of world.

Erin Mackenzie (13)
Coleraine High School

CHALK

Have you ever seen a person
Who looked at a piece of chalk?
Who has ever cared what it looked like
In its fancy Crayola box?

Chalk has always been there
Since the start of time.
Maybe some great man used chalk
To draw his very first line!

We use it on our blackboards,
And even when we speak, yet
I don't know how something useful like chalk
Became compared with cheese?

I'm sure if it had feelings,
It would be very bored.
Scribbling, circling and writing things
Up and down a blackboard.

I'm sure that it would like a change
Instead of writing all day long.
It might want to be an actor or an astronaut
Or be able to sing a song.

I think that sometimes chalk
Gets tired of drawing everything.
So someday why don't you try
Drawing it for a change!

So next time you see a piece of chalk,
Don't just throw it away
Think about how the chalk feels
And use it for one more day!

Deepa Varghese (13)
Coleraine High School

ORANGE

On the tree they hang
Like golden drops of honey,
Suspended in mid-air.
Once ripe, the yellow darkens
Into a rich orange
Like autumn leaves.
That ostentatious orange shines
Like a lamp in the dark.
Glossy, rough skin,
Sprinkled with dimples,
Meets my hand as I
Pull it from the tree.
I hold this misshapen tennis ball,
Cold to touch and yet,
Looks as warm as the sun.
The tough skin protects
The jewel inside.
I open the chest of gold,
Each segment shaped like
A veiny, orange moon,
Covered in white cloud.
Sharp daggers pierce my nose
As I take a whiff of the smell.
The tangy juice fills my mouth
As I bite into the flesh.
Soon, after a few chews
It is gone.
All that is left is a coiled skin
Rather like a small, sleeping snake.

Emma Cummings (13)
Coleraine High School

DAD

Listen to the wind sing, Dad,
The blue-eyed little boy murmurs;
Do you hear its lonely melody?
Why does it sound so sad?

See how the butterflies dance, Dad,
The blue-eyed little boy says;
They look so pretty on the roses,
Why do they have to fly away?

Look at the stars shimmer, Dad,
The blue-eyed little boy sighs;
They sparkle like Mum's eyes used to,
Do they too have to die?

You hear the bluebells chiming, Dad,
The blue-eyed little boy whispers;
They sound a little bit glum,
Do they also miss their mum?

Feel the raindrops on your face, Dad?
The blue-eyed little boy asks;
I know your cheeks were already wet,
Do you have to hide behind a mask?

See how the sun's peeking out, Dad?
The blue-eyed little boy smiles;
The yellow rays make everything better, Dad,
It all just takes a while.
Please don't cry any more, Dad,
You have to let go of the pain,
Losing Mum was tough, Dad,
But someday you'll smile again . . .

Bella Huang (15)
Coleraine High School

THAT APPLE

Sitting there
Saying eat me please, eat me
But if I do I won't have room for my tea.

With your
Glossy, green, tempting skin
I just have to give in.

When I take
The first bite you go crunch
And your tasty juice comes oozing out.

Your flesh was
Cold, fresh and soft,
The name of *that apple* will linger on.

Once I started
To eat I just could not stop
For the taste has captured me.

I hit something
Hard and it didn't taste nice
It was your fat core that held your seedlings.

Then you were finished and I was sad
But then I realised that your taste had lingered on,
And my hands from that day's feast
Were sticky with your juice and
My hands smelt of your smell,
That smell I still can't
Describe,
That apple smell.

Stacey Wilmot (14)
Coleraine High School

MOONLIT SKY

It turns night,
And I watch the moon
Appearing still in
The dark sky.

       It's glistening reflection
       Falls on the lake,
       With a peaceful
       But eerie effect.

Why is the sun so
Bright and brings warmth?
Yet the moon is dull
And brings cold.

       The sun gives,
       The moon takes,
       They're so different
       But yet the same.

The moon has phases
The sun does not
Why? We ask
The truth is locked.

Jenna Emo (14)
Coleraine High School

IN MY DREAMS

In my dreams
The cars are stars
That drive across the sky.

In my dreams
I'm in a balloon
Trying to reach the moon.

And up I float
On my magic boat
Across the cloudy sea.

Look at me I yell and shout
I'm free, I'm free
Gently flying free.

Lauren McCracken (12)
Coleraine High School

IF ONLY . . .

If only snow was warm
It would be like a fluffy Heaven.
I could lie outside for hours
Sinking my hands into the cotton wool like whiteness.

If only I had wings
Then I would feel free,
When I soar up through the sky
And dance on the dreamy clouds.

If only animals could talk
I could ask where my cat goes at night,
Why do cows sleep standing?
And are sheep really that stupid?

Life is full of 'If onlys'
If only my pen did my homework for me.
If only sweets were good for my teeth.
If only the weekends were longer.
If only . . .
If only . . .
If only . . .
All you can do is dream.

Christine Wallace (14)
Coleraine High School

SNOW

What words do you think of and what pictures do you see?
Christmas, a warm glowing fire,
With cards on the mantelpiece,
A Christmas tree tall and proud,
Out through the window we see all is white,
And a snowman standing alone.

Or do you see that it's cold and harsh?
Only there to block the roads
Freeze the pipes and causing us to stay in the house.

I think it's starts off pure,
Only touched by the hand that rolled it over the land,
And gentle sprinkles snowflakes across the top,
As a mother would sprinkle icing sugar over the icing on a cake.

Until,
We start to tramp, stump, shovel, throw and drive through
Ruining the smooth glistening surface,
We break it down to slippy, sliding slush,
Not crispy white now a murky brown.

Maybe,
At the next sunrise,
We open the curtains to find,
The hand has rolled and sprinkled
Our world is white again.

Elaine McGeehan (14)
Coleraine High School

THE KIWI FRUIT

The kiwi may have a strange furry skin
But it is mostly succulent within,
To eat it you must peel it first,
It really does quench your thirst.

The lime green flesh is soft and sweet
On your spoon, a mouth-watering treat
Eat alone or with ice cream
This spongy fruit is just a dream.

Laura Thompson (14)
Coleraine High School

ONLY IF!

Only if I didn't get up today,
I wouldn't have gone to school.
Then I wouldn't have gone to English,
And I wouldn't have got in trouble.

Only if I didn't get in trouble,
I wouldn't have cried.
Then everyone wouldn't have laughed at me,
And I wouldn't have faked a sicky.

Only if I didn't fake a sicky,
Then my mum wouldn't have had to come for me.
Then she wouldn't have found out the truth,
And she wouldn't have been so angry.

Only if my mum wasn't so angry,
She wouldn't have broke the good plates,
Or burnt the dinner,
Or even burnt the curtains.

Only if the curtains didn't catch fire,
Then we would've got to the phone in time.
Then we would've called the fire brigade,
Then our house wouldn't have disappeared into ashes.

Only if it hadn't happened.

Sarah McNicholl (14)
Coleraine High School

CLOUDS

They're fluffy like cotton wool,
They're wispy like candyfloss
There are a lot of different shapes
If you look hard enough you can see almost anything,
A boat, a tree or even a fish.

They are all different colours,
White, grey, black,
They are full of water
And they change with the weather.

Clouds,
What are they?

Where did they come from?

Why are they there?

What is their purpose?

Melanie McKeeman (13)
Coleraine High School

AUTUMN

The green hands that waved at you,
Have turned red, gold and brown.
As they wave for the last time,
They prepare for their fall.

As quiet as a ballerina,
They twirl and dance in the air.
Round and round they go,
Like a washing machine.

As they lie on the ground,
Like a patchwork quilt
They rustle as people bustle,
Through the busy street.

They now lie in solitude,
And wonder why the people never waved.
They feel alone and forgotten
They're swept away and the story begins again.

Claire McNabb (14)
Coleraine High School

SNOWFLAKES

Each one is different,
But somehow the same.
From up above in the winter sky
The snowflakes plummet to the earth like a waterfall.

Flakes of glitter,
Blanket the trees
Falling down in clusters of white
How I love to watch the snowflakes tumble down.

I often wonder,
Why and what do they mean?
Who made these beautiful falling stars
And where do they come from?

To me they're a sign of winter bliss,
And He who's up above
We thank Him for the snowflakes
His glistering winter rain.

Claire Stevenson (13)
Coleraine High School

NECTARINE

Sphere-shaped like a tennis ball although it doesn't bounce.
Smells like a dark red rose in the autumn breeze.
Autumn colours - yellow, red and orange blended into one.
As silent as a mourning man.
Sweet, succulent, smooth, shiny and silent sphere,
Sitting in a bowl of different colours and textures.
I raise the tennis ball to my mouth,
My teeth suddenly attack,
As if I were a soaring eagle who had just spotted its prey.
Crunch, I tear a chunk off and leave a hollow mark,
Tossing and turning like clothes in a washing machine,
I munch until I can swallow.
I take another bite; the autumn colours disappear,
An oval hard stone is revealed.
Only one mouthful left . . .
Now it's gone.
Left with a stone and a sweet after taste in my mouth.
That was tasty! Ummm!

Andrea Flatt (14)
Coleraine High School

SNOWFLAKES

Snowflakes glistening,
Shaped like spider's webs.
Dancing in the air,
For all to see,
Falling on the cold, crisp ground.

As the light shimmers on them,
They twist and turn,
With a certain type of elegance,
As they stand on their own.

Looking for someone to be their friend,
Everyone stops to admire,
Gazing at them,
But just pass by in their busy lives.

Laura Clyde (13)
Coleraine High School

THE FIGHT FOR SURVIVAL

I lie in my bed at night
Wondering, hoping, praying,
If I'll be able to open my eyes the following morning,
And continue on with my life.

With flash backs from the news,
Racing through my mind,
So many questions,
Not enough answers.

Dreaming of aeroplanes in the sky,
Just gliding into those buildings,
Within minutes they just flutter to the ground like a young bird
                                        learning to fly
Leaving thousands to mourn the death of their loved ones.

Now it's time for retaliation,
Time to get even
Leaving thousands of helpless people homeless
To starve to death.

Then I get up in the morning,
I survived the previous night,
But it wasn't all a dream,
It's reality!

Ellen McDowell (13)
Coleraine High School

FEAR

The room is spinning all around me
Muffled voice, blurred faces.
Faster and faster, gaining speed
I think I'm falling
My trembling body finds a chair
Into which it gladly sinks.

What do the others think?
Why does it bother me?
Why am I scared of them?
Why are there such cruel people in the world?
Why do I not find it funny?

I'm going to have to face
This monster
Silent but deadly it will take
A grip on my life.

I stand up.
The room slows down
One foot in front of the other,
I stumble across the room,
Towards the door.
The room gives a slight wobble,
I don't care
I'm free from the monster's clutch
For now . . .

Susan Brown (13)
Coleraine High School

NEW YORK

New York morning
Just another day
People wake up
Merry and gay.

All went to work
Looking their best
The day the same
As all the rest.

The joy of the day
Did suddenly flee
As sorrow and grief
Became their enemy.

Hijacked planes
On a mission of hate
Struck the twin towers
And sealed their fate.

Policemen and firemen
To the rescue made haste
To help the poor people
Trapped and encased.

But many a life
Was lost on that day
Never again
To be merry and gay.

Vicki McConaghie (12)
Coleraine High School

My Dog

My dog with its fluffy white coat with brown spots,
She runs as if she is gliding through the air,
The friendly wag of her tail,
The tired patter after running through a field
The excitement when she sees dinner in her bowl,
Her lick so soft and gentle
She sunbathes on a warm summer's day
Her rustling through the leaves in a forest on a cold autumn night
She comes home so white,
No sight of her brown spots after running through the snow
You brush her clean then the wagging of her tail as she gets a treat
She chases the birds and rabbits as she glides through the park
                                    on a warm spring day
My dog is pure and simply the best of all dogs.

Ruth Stewart (13)
Coleraine High School

The Apple

This fruit makes its journey alone,
All its friends are away, somewhere in the world,
It's not like the banana or the grape,
They have friends who are always there,
The lonely apple is then in someone's fruit bowl,
With other species alone like it,
Then a man comes over and picks up the fruit
And with a hard crunch, he tears a bit off the apple
With hard, strong, white warriors,
He tears off another bit and he keeps on going until the core,
The man wipes off the sweet juice at his mouth and says
'That was a jolly good apple.'
The apple's life has now come to an end.

Cheryl McIntyre (13)
Coleraine High School

THIS TRANQUIL PLACE

This tranquil place,
Where the soft gentle breeze sweeps through,
Stems and branches move to and fro,
And leaves dance and birds sing.
The rosy petals stir in the warm breeze,
And the colours blur as stems entwine.
Sweet fragrances fill the air and become entangled in a perfumed
web of spring.
Emerald weeds sprout up from the petal covered floor.
This private place is hidden by the cold harsh walls,
But inside there is a placid, soothing atmosphere,
Where on a chair sits a solitary shape,
As he enjoys this tranquil place.

Sarah Harkness (14)
Coleraine High School

A SUMMER'S SOLACE

Fleecy, white clouds move majestically
Through the baby blue sky.
Underneath this rooftop
The marble green ocean spews milky foam
Over the sandy beach.
Large, black rocks like sea turtles
Rest on the sand,
And are baked by the glaring sun.
Children play and are engulfed
By the waters of the vast ocean.
Human laughter and the cries of birds
Are heard in the salty air.
Black, domineering cliffs in the distance
Jealously guard this tranquil scene.

Rhonda Boyd (15)
Coleraine High School

RAIN IS LIKE . . .

Rain is like confetti
Falling from the sky.
It opens up our memories
Of happy days gone by.

It never stops to amaze me
Especially in summer time,
When it hits the layer of
Freshly sewn grass
It lies like a blanket
On the ground.

The rays of the sun are
Like beams from Heaven
Soaking up the rain that lies like confetti
On the ground.
Those happy memories of days gone by,
Suddenly float away like angels wings
On a couple's happy day.

Just like confetti, rain comes in all shapes,
Sizes and forms.
As I look from my bedroom window
Those happy memories spring to mind.

Janine Henry (13)
Coleraine High School

AUTUMN

Leaves turn brown,
They all fall down,
Signs of autumn are all around.

Dark and dreary nights are on their way,
Nothing to do,
No time to play.

Autumn can be lots of fun,
Kicking the leaves
As they fall off the trees.

When autumn goes,
Winter appears
And it won't be back
For another year.

Susan Kirkpatrick (12)
Coleraine High School

A WORLD AT WAR

Sitting, watching the moon
As it drifts dreamily from behind a cloud.
Everything is fine, everything is calm.
Then comes the distant crack of gunfire
And the sudden jerk back to reality.
Everything is not fine, everything is not calm.
This world is at war.

Lives destroyed, families torn apart,
Wondering if death is just around the corner.
The many questions to which there are no answers.
In one short day, 24 little hours life will be permanently changed.
Parents once yelled and argued, not any more.
Children once screamed in excitement and anger, now death.
Again we are reminded this world is at war.

Sitting, watching the moon
As it drifts dreamily from behind a cloud.
A fighter plane is suddenly silhouetted against the huge silver orb
Suspended in the velvety, blue sky.
The surreal image is shattered,
This world is at war.

Kelly Thompson (13)
Coleraine High School

LOVE

The first time I saw you
My head felt all light
I knew my love was true
It felt so right.

You're so cute and so sweet
I had fancied you for so long
Every time our eyes meet
You always act strong.

Oh, how I love you Gaz
I always think of you
Even in maths,
I know my love is true.

I will love you forever
You will always be in my heart
We will never, ever
Grow apart!

Simone Young (12)
Coleraine High School

THE EYE OF THE STORM

A dark, raging cloud hangs,
As the terrifying tornado is set on its destructive path,
Uprooting and dismantling as it rolls along,
Causing havoc and fear to nature and mankind,
Piteous and motionless life below,
Cannot compete with its overwhelming power,
Light is blocked because of the thick lining in the sky,
No one can be seen or heard,
Except the roar of the fierce wind.

Caroline Keys (14)
Coleraine High School

A Baby's Mind

I look out all around me,
And don't understand what I see.
Being passed from lap to lap,
When all I want is a nice long nap.

Getting toys shoved in my face,
People running all over the place.
Why can't they all just go away
And give me peace on my first day?

People around me in every space,
Poking fingers in my face.
I wish that this would all be by,
Yep, I think it's time to cry.

Someone throws me in the air,
Another waves a teddy bear.
Grannies and aunties crying with glee,
You'd think they were the babies, not me!

Rachel McAllister (14)
Coleraine High School

Precious Tears

Small, defenceless, weak, so unaware.
Tears leave her deep brown eyes, following their usual course.
She feels no pain, yet agony stabs her unknowing heart
- A pain deeper than I can tell.
She feels lonely, unloved - but not for long.
Her precious face looks to the sky and her last tear falls.
she is alone no more.

Rebecca Cochrane (15)
Coleraine High School

INSIDE MUM'S HEAD

Have they done their homework?
Time they were going to school,
Need a cup of coffee.

Sunny beach in Spain,
Escaping from it all,
Need a glass of wine.

What will I cook for tea?
Where's the cat?
Need a lie down.

Where's the iron?
Better go to Sylvia's,
Need an assistant.

Kathryn McCullagh (14)
Coleraine High School

MY FAVOURITE PLACE

My garden is a lovely place,
Where I can run and play
When Mam and Dad say 'Come inside.'
Outside I'd rather stay.

We have a great big beech tree
In autumn leaves do fall
Reds and golds come floating free
Upon the grassy ground.

The cat she hides from Prince the dog
Behind the trees and flowers,
And watches for a little mouse
For hours and hours and hours.

Christine Gilmore (12)
Coleraine High School

MY BROTHERS' MINDS

We like to fight,
All day, all night.
With each other,
Or with our mother.

Just out of spite,
We turn off the light
On our sister,
Who is a pester.

Homework is a synch,
'Cause we get our mum to do every inch.
At the end of it all we go to bed,
As our eyes turn to lead.

Next morning is the same,
And the cycle starts again!

Adrienne-Ann Scott (14)
Coleraine High School

AUTUMN

Crimson, golden and orange leaves,
Gently falling in the breeze.
Chestnuts falling in the trees,
Autumn is here for all to see.
The wind is fierce when I fly my kite,
It soars in the sky with all its might.
Red berries on the bushes for me to pick,
Blackberry pie is a treat.
Blustery winds make the leaves swirl around my feet,
Crackle, crackle, crackle as they fall under my feet.

Arlene Boyd (13)
Coleraine High School

SUMMER GOES

Summer goes, summer goes
Like last year it shall come back
The salty sea flows
With the sun it shall attack
Until next year winter comes
With the frost and the snow.

Summer brought, summer brought
All the sunshine burning hot
Nice, fluffy, warm sand
Working hard to get a tan
White ice cream and swimming pools
Ice lollies nice and cool.

Summer took, summer took
Dreaded maths and physics books
I'll enjoy my play
Until they return one day
September creeps up fast
Why can't summer last?

Lauren Campbell (12)
Coleraine High School

AUTUMN

Summer season over,
Autumn just begun.
Leaves changing colour,
From green to red and brown.

Leaves are falling,
Trees look bare.
Footpaths are coloured,
The crunch of leaves fills the air.

Mornings are dawning later,
The air is getting cooler.
Clouds are growing heavy,
The nights are drawing in late.

Rachel Campbell (12)
Coleraine High School

WHEN THE WORLD SHED A TEAR

Tuesday morning,
An uneasy silence,
Something not quite right.

Open the curtains,
What a surprise
Looks like the middle of the night.

Downstairs I go,
Mom and Dad crying,
This can't be right.

TV screen,
Flashes disaster,
The buildings set alight.

All too familiar,
So near, but why?
What a sight!

What a day,
Shed a tear
I will try with all my might.

Nicola Platt (12)
Coleraine High School

SECOND WORLD

This world, ancient but new,
Timeless yet living,
Abandoned yet found.
Air around is moist and heavy,
With a scent of freshness
Enclosed from the outside world.
A canopy of playful leaves,
A floor of damp green grass,
And walls of khaki tree trunks.
Only a selected few are privileged,
To unlock the door to this world,
And lock it behind them.
The air unbroken,
Is cut through by the wings of a bird,
So gracefully,
Like scissors through paper
For a place perceived as soundless,
It is stirring with speech.
The whispering of the motioned leaves
Voices of the birds replying.
Shushing of the wind,
From time to time does come.
Now I hear my call to return,
To hustle and bustle,
And all things lifeless.

Katie Eardley (14)
Coleraine High School

WHAT IS IT?

As I see them sitting there,
Like buds in May about
To burst into flower,
Glistening green like,
A bunch of emeralds.

As the sun shines on them,
I can see the veins shining though,
Like little roads all intertwined within this one matter.

I look, hardly daring to move,
Than I do,
I walk forward, approaching this wonderful,
Creation and look closer at
The green objects, I pick one up.

Without the will to destroy, I put one in,
My mouth as I clamp my jaws together,
Like a miniature bomb.

The shiny outer green surface,
  Explodes
Revealing a delicious, sweet, fleshy interior.

I swirl it around in my mouth and swallow,
It's gone,
Cautiously I pick another,
And start the process again,
Now I know these bell like things, they are,
  Grapes.

Arlene O'Neill (13)
Coleraine High School

THE ODD FRUIT

A journey to an exotic place
An attraction making your heart race
A loud thump as the heavy object reached the ground
I ran to the place where I found
A soft, but firm yellow ball
Was this what made that fall?
I think I could hear it call, calling my name
Calling me closer, but no closer I came.
As the sharp, bitter scent filled the air
The sight so beautiful and yet so rare
The outside, the colour of the sun,
The inside of a severed thumb
Spilling out streams of early rouge summer wine
The taste of sherbet, I'm glad this fruit is mine!
Colour like the orange, its outer suit
A wonderful fruit is the grapefruit.

Amy Gamble (13)
Coleraine High School

DRUIDS

Since time memorial and forever
Past and present join together
On midsummer's night the druids come,
To worship round their sacred stones.
They hold their banners depicting scenes
Of simple shapes and things which have been.
Dressed in white against the dark oppressing stones
All you can hear are their soft soulful tones,
Until the sky becomes bright,
And the chants grow slight,
And nothing is left of the cult in the night.

Suzanne Boyd (14)
Coleraine High School

A GIRL'S HEAD

Inside a girl's head there
Is a brain that has
Boys, boys, boys going around in it.
In town she spies a cute boy,
And inside her head she thinks,
Is my hair OK?
Is my make-up OK?
What are my clothes like?
At home she thinks,
Are my parents ever
Gonna stop nagging at me?
Is my little brother gonna ever,
Stop annoying me?
When she is on her own she thinks,
Where are my family and
Friends when I need them?

Shona McAfee (13)
Coleraine High School

CHRISTMAS

Christmas trees and decorations,
Lights that sparkle bright.
Snow outside covering everything,
Glimmering and shining white.
Snowmen in every garden,
Each with a different coloured scarf.
Christmas dinner is always yummy,
Christmas pudding fills your tummy.
Families meeting,
To enjoy this festive season.

Victoria McCahon (13)
Coleraine High School

HORSES

With her long, graceful legs,
She slowly paces round,
Eating the sweet meadow grass.
As I open the field gate,
She lifts her long, silvery neck,
And canters over and nuzzles my pocket.
She neighs with delight,
As I slip the halter over her soft, velvety nose.
Then I climb onto her broad back,
And off we go.
I feel her mane gently brush my face,
As we gallop towards the rising sun.
I love horses.
Don't you?

Hannah McKay (12)
Coleraine High School

THE CITY

The city is a wondrous place.
The blaring of horns and buzzing of people
Let us know it's still breathing.
Skyscrapers stretch up to Heaven
Like trees growing towards the light.
The streets are crowded with engines
That choke the earth with their fumes.
Even the water is buzzing
With the wake of the boats
And the swishing movement of the waves,
As they bash against the sides of them.
It shimmers and glistens in the sunlit sky.

Gillian McNeill (14)
Coleraine High School

PAIN

Questions float inside my head
Asking you why you did it?
What ifs linger?
Your actions have caused piercing pains
That spin frantically inside me,
Like a whirlpool - never ceasing.
An internal vicious circle.
Stinging tears flow from my eyes,
Like a river.
In everything I do, in everything I say,
There is a reminder of you.
Will the burning pain ever ease?
People say, 'With time.'
But, the love I have for you will last,
Longer than eternity.
No! The pain will never cease?

Amy Grissam (16)
Coleraine High School

EMERALD HILLS

Snow white mountains stand to attention,
Protecting the tranquillity of emerald green hills.
The placid lake rests in the valley of green,
Staring up at the light blue sky
At it rises high above the grassy hills.
A crystal clear stream meanders its way through the grass
And enters the aquamarine lake unheard.
The fresh air is sweetly fragranced by the wild flowers,
Fuschia, sky blue, violet and orange
This land is so peaceful and silent,
Isolated from the rest of the world.

Keira Dinsmore (14)
Coleraine High School

THE FOREST

In a single moment, we trudged towards the leafy, ochre door,
and stepped through.

The splendour, the beauty - the wonderment
Of our newly found treasure.

Great branches sweep upwards,
Their finger - like projections
Point in the direction of destiny.
We stand motionless,
Feeling their cool breath enthral us
And press against our faces.

We listen to the winged carnivores,
Chirruping in their emerald belfries,
Worshipping their green, foliate, masters.

The soft 'shush' of the colourless giver of life,
Radiates tranquillity and joy,
As it splashes on the moist earth
Before it.

The sweet scent of the petite flower,
Spreads its perfume
In a hazy mist,
Mingling with the vitality,
In this mystical land.

The harmonious aura of nature
Smothers and draws us
Into safety and security.
Our world is at peace
And is still once more.

Quiet,
Silent,
Still.

Jayne Thompson (14)
Coleraine High School

MOMENT BEFORE DEATH

Beep, beep, beep, beep
Faces: family, friends and foes.
Will I make it? No one knows.
At six years old I'm on my bike,
Doing exactly as I like.
Standing there all dressed in white,
But the lights are fading; it's not so bright.
Memories all come flooding back
Fading slightly, as breath I lack.
Graduation, Mum's so proud,
To see my children's not allowed.
I'm getting older; life takes its strain,
It's all mixed up, I'm three again.
Life seems not to even care
When to death I finally stare.
Slipping quietly away,
Life will not give another day.

Alison Wallace (16)
Coleraine High School

WINTER

Winter is here, the cold weather has come,
No more sunny spells now
Just snow and ice around,
Lying thickly on the ground.

The snowman stands in the garden,
With his hat and scarf as clothes.
With an orange carrot for his nose,
And daddy's slippers for his toes.

Long, dark, winter days,
The wind, the rain and the snow
At last we see the Christmas lights
Not long before spring's in sight.

Kelly-Anne Glenn (12)
Coleraine High School

THE GREAT CITY

Powerful city,
Centre of trade,
That New York's Twin Towers
Should fall in a raid!

Thousands of lives
Lost in the rubble
Who would have thought
Of such terrible trouble?

So many lives lost,
So many tears shed,
So many last calls home,
Who can count the cost?

Esther Reid (12)
Coleraine High School

AUTUMN

Leaves swirl past the window
When the north winds blow
The memories of summer
Have gone long ago.

The hedgerows are thinning
The trees are all bare,
The owls sit on branches,
Wide-eyed, they stare.

The harvest is plentiful
The children all run,
To the bonfires and fireworks
Which add to the fun.

Cara Fullerton (12)
Coleraine High School

INSIDE A TYPICAL GIRL'S HEAD

In it there is a shopping mall
And a plan to get that boy
She really must have.

And there is school
Which should come first
But somehow never does.

And there are worries like
What will I wear to the party?
Does my bum look big in my new dress?
And of course was that piece of gossip I heard today really true?

Trudy Harkness (13)
Coleraine High School

NEW YEAR'S RESOLUTIONS

I'll try to be pleasant to my brother,
Even when he is not pleasant to me.
I will stop hiding his bed time teddy,
And then selling it back for 20p!
For Mum, I will part my hair to the side,
Even though the middle looks best!
I won't read (under torch light) to midnight,
And be exhausted for my English test.
When helping Dad grout the cement in his wall,
I won't moan about the state of my hands.
If he wants to show off in the kitchen,
I'll surprise him by washing the pans.
When my big sister has friends in her room,
I'll not complain or be jealous or shout.
I won't hide under her bed for hours,
And tell everyone what they talked about.
My family they've noticed the change in me,
Glad I've grown up . . . but they haven't heard -
My best resolution is yet to come -
These only last till January 3rd!

Danielle Brown (12)
Coleraine High School

MY ENDLESS JOURNEY

I travel around the Earth
A ball of green and blue
But from where I watch with the stars up high
I see pain and sorrow, fear and terror,
Actions which cause me to wonder,
How much longer will the Earth need the sun?

Joanna Morrell (12)
Coleraine High School

A Winter Spot

Alone, walking amongst the trees
Standing tall, bare and vulnerable
Since autumn departed
The stillness of winter fills the air
As I move I feel the silence
The peaceful calm of this wondrous place
I stop, no one else just me
The only sound is the soft crunch of snow beneath my feet.
I've started again
I'm the only movement
Full of life, yet nothing stirs
Everything is quiet
Time has passed and night approaches,
The sun starts to set in the amethyst sky
A warm glow of light streaked across it
I must leave now
I take one last look
This is beautiful.

Amy Ballance (15)
Coleraine High School

Armageddon

As I enter the unknown I find it unique,
The violent war has ended but the remnants are still in mourning,
No remedy can heal this sorrow,
Mortals trudge along in desolation and despondency,
The streets are paved with litter.
Ashen and murky, the skies are monochromatic,
The musty, damp smell is so pungent
I feel as though I have just swallowed it.
Famine surrounds me.

Katherine Campbell (14)
Coleraine High School

OUR WORLD TODAY

When you look at the world today, what do you see?
People crying, people dying,
What has happened to you and me?

People don't have food to eat or a place to learn,
All over the world these things are happening,
Which should cause us concern.

There are so many problems which need to be solved,
And can be if we,
Get involved.

Together we could succeed,
To help those people,
Who are in need.

If only we would play our part,
We could bring help to those
With a heavy heart.

Catherine Black (12)
Coleraine High School

SURPRISES

Surprises are such wonderful things,
Great happiness, they always bring.
Childrens' faces fill with joy
When they receive their favourite toys.

Sometimes I wonder what I will get,
Perhaps a scarf or a knitted hat?
Is the box big or is it small?
Is it round or is it tall?

Disappointment sometimes arrives,
When Gran makes you a pair of pink trousers.
But when you see what your brother gets
You're glad you got your trousers, I bet!

Sara Caithness (13)
Coleraine High School

THE DAY AMERICA SUFFERED

September 11th started as a bright autumn day
People going about their daily business,
Suddenly the calmness all changed into utter chaos,
One building then two burst into flames and then collapsed,
People ran screaming to get out of these buildings,
What hope had they? None, no none at all!

Some were lying trapped and badly hurt,
Emergency services running through the carnage,
Trying to find anyone lucky enough to have survived,
But, oh so few were they.

Little children asking for their mummies and daddies,
Had they lived or died?
Adults searching in vain for their loved ones,
Had they lived or died?

The world watched in horror and dismay as the people of America
suffered,
All that anyone could ask was, *why, oh why?*
So God Bless America and take into His loving care
All the people affected,
The day America suffered.

Janet Warke (12)
Coleraine High School

HALLOWE'EN

On the 31st October
It all turns dark and eerie,
Gazing at the moon,
Shadows sweep across.

Walking down the alleyway
Cats screeching,
Witches cackling,
Hurry and get home.

Fireworks,
Trick or treat,
Fancy dress
And lots of sweets.

Just one thing
I have to say
Hallowe'en
Is on its way.

Joanne McIlreavy (12)
Coleraine High School

APPLE

It hung,
One of many moons,
Until plucked from its universe,
Large and diverse.

Its red and freckled skin
Is rough against my tongue.
I taste its sweet flesh,
Succulent and fresh.

A mini galaxy
Of glistening stars
Lies in its core.
My taste buds cry out for more.

This wonderful galaxy
Eventually withers and dies,
Yet another disappearing planet
In the depths of the skies.

Katie Adams (13)
Coleraine High School

INSIDE OUTER SPACE

A bunch of crazy comets
Creatures from a different place,
A group of poor, lost astronauts,
Inside outer space.

An apple from Apollo
A totally different race,
A black hole near Uranus,
Inside outer space.

Cool little red moon buggies,
On Mars having a race,
But I have pole position,
Inside outer space.

Even thought it's fun out there,
I really like my place,
I think that I would rather have Earth
Than inside outer space!

Samantha Vickery (12)
Coleraine High School

A GIRL'S HEAD

If you were inside a girl's head you would get lost
There are many roads and junctions to each part of her brain!
There is one to 'boys' and 'hair' and 'clothes' and 'make-up'
And lots more that her head will soon explode
If there are any more parts added!

Girls daydream about boys all day long and never stop
And even at night they dream about them!
I should know because I am one,
And I must admit, I'm like that too!

Girl's love to go shopping and buy new clothes
They also love the colour pink as that describes what they are like,
It means that they are sweet, innocent and always little angels
(That doesn't mean that we can't let our hair down and have some fun!)

So as I finish this poem I just want to leave you with this verse
'What are little girls made of, made of?
What are little girls made of?
Sugar and spice and all things nice,
That's what little girls are made of!'

Rachel McClure (13)
Coleraine High School

GRAPEFRUIT

A yellow-orange skin with pink flesh inside,
A quarter slice of grapefruit I see before my eyes.
A smell so sour and acrid,
A vision of sunset at low tide.

As I peel back the bitter, fresh fruit
From the bumpy, tough skin
I see a furry white layer
Pale, dry and thin.

It has tiny little seeds, no bigger than a pin head
It tastes like its smell, so harsh
Once all the insides have been torn off,
There is only a patchy white and peachy coloured mess of goo!

Bryoney-Jayne Cromie (13)
Coleraine High School

THE APPLE

Under an old apple tree, there lies the treasured fruit,
Scarred from its fall like a wounded man of war.
It's a discoloured green-yellow tarnished with red,
Which droops down from the top.
Staining as it weeps, like the tears of a grieving child.
Its rounded edges and plump little body
So sleek and tender to see.

It felt frosty and bleak like a cold winter's morning,
Glazed like an ice skater's dream.
The pleasure I consumed, as my teeth tore the skin,
Then dug into the pale succulent flesh.
All you could hear was the crunch of the apple,
The rippling of the wind through the trees,
Whistling with every little breeze.

The mouth-watering taste I hoped would never end,
But soon the flesh turned brown.
It became discoloured like a leaf in autumn,
And dry like desert drought.
Now I'm left waiting for the big, old, apple tree to blossom,
That I have no doubt.

Karen Newton (13)
Coleraine High School

The Trip Of A Lifetime

The trip of a lifetime seems so far away,
But when the time comes I'll be glad.
For when I climb aboard that Boeing 747,
I'll be on my way to Florida.

A villa is there with our name on it,
From the tenth to the twenty-fourth of August.
I'll miss all my pets and of course my friends
But I definitely won't miss chores!

Disneyland, Universal Studios and more,
All these places to go.
Two whole weeks will not be enough but,
I'm sure it'll be fine for me.

When the twenty-fourth of August comes around,
I'll be sad but glad at the same time.
Sad because the holiday is over,
Glad because I'm going home to my nice warm bed!

Amanda McIntyre (12)
Coleraine High School

Inside My Mum's Head

Inside my mum's head
There is colour and vision
Everything is beauty and light
Nothing is dead.

Inside my mum's head
There is friends and family,
Parties and work.
Has the cat been fed?

Inside my mum's head
There is clothes, make-up,
Her weight, her shoes,
Her bed.

But most important
As she tells me often
In her head is . . .
Me!

Poppy Warwicker (13)
Coleraine High School

INSIDE MY HEAD

In it there is make-up, clothes and shoes,
And a plan for getting money off my dad.

And there are boys,
Lots of boys.

And there is a list of clothes I want
A list of CDs
And new shoes from Top Shop.

There is a swimming gala,
A hockey match.
My horse and dog,
And my best friends too.

There are lots of important things too, like,
Does he notice me?
Do I look alright?
Is my hair and make-up perfect?
What will I wear?
There is so much to think about.

Lesley Davis (13)
Coleraine High School

AUTUMN

Summer days have come and gone,
Leave have fallen on the lawn.
Birds migrate from far and near,
The whistling wind says autumn is here.

Shorter day and darker nights,
Hibernation hides the light.
Hedges full of hips and haws,
Squirrels with acorns in their paws.

Harvest time and back to school,
Grey skies, it's getting cool.
Crunching leaves beneath my feet,
Apples ripen ready to eat.

Children gathering berries and seeds,
The outdoor life that's all they need.
All too soon it's come and gone,
Winter is near and soon will dawn.

Katherine Minihan (12)
Coleraine High School

APPLES

Grown from the Garden of Eden,
Passed down from each generation,
Another apple has finally ripened
Giving off it's soft red glow.
It's round in shape and hard to touch.

Apples, some are sweet, some are bitter
They come in different colours too,
Green, red, russet,
You'll find one to suit you.

Take one crunchy bite,
And to much of a delight,
You will find the core holding those
Seeds, to grow a new family.
So go on, take an apple a day
And keep that doctor away.

Abigail McNeill (13)
Coleraine High School

ROUND ABOUT YEAR

Spring is a time when lambs skip and play,
Tiny new buds appear on the trees.
The birds come back from lands a far
And the days grow gradually longer.

In summer you hear the birds chirping high up in the trees
Children splash in the warm blue seas
Flowers bloom into beautiful colours
While freshly cut grass fragrances the air.

In autumn the wind howls,
Animals store up their homes for cold days to come
Leaves fall off the trees
And the night draws in shorter.

In winter children build their snowmen white,
While adults put up their Christmas lights.
The little robin looks for food
Everyone enjoys the good this Christmas brings out in people.

Sarah McMullan (12)
Coleraine High School

THE GARDEN PARADISE

Placid air surrounds me,
Sub-tropical heat induces weariness,
A myriad of scents
Confuse my senses.
I am enclosed by a rainbow of colour
As sunlight streams through the tree tops
The nature that surrounds me is
Untouched by human hands.
The hidden paradise's beauty amazes me
The birds sing happily
And fill me with joy,
When I hear their beautiful sound.
The leaves rustle and the water gently
Glides over the rocks making a sound which is
Relaxing and gives a sense of calmness.
The water in the stream trickles softly
And moves elegantly and with ease.
The site before me reminds me of a paradise
Where nature is all around me.

Zara Stewart (14)
Coleraine High School

AUTUMN

Summer has gone, autumn has come with the breeze
Leaves in many colours drift down from the trees.
The days get shorter, the air colder
Apples fall from the tree and moulder.

Woodland creatures store nuts away
While farmers toil to bring in the hay.
Birds line up on telephone wires
Cattle look forward to the warmth of the byre.

Summer flowers no more are seen.
Yellows and russets replace the green.
Berries ripen in the hedgerow
Hips and haws and the purple sloe.

Fiona Hill (12)
Coleraine High School

THE WIND

In the spring there is a light wind
With a slight chill,
So the pretty flowers aren't touched,
Everything is calm and peaceful,
And everything grows again and there are new beginnings.

In the summer there is no wind,
But there are blistering heat waves,
The sun shines down and lights up the world,
Which creates a scorching heat.

In the autumn there are blustery winds,
Which blow the leaves off the trees,
Twisting and twirling a tornado of leaves,
The rainbow of colour is magical.

In the winter the wind is strong and fearsome,
It has a spine-tingling chill,
I love to wrap up warm,
To keep out the chills and sneezes.

Amy Watton (13)
Coleraine High School

LOST

Far away from home,
I'm lost
Even though I'm troubled I stop to gaze
Tall mountains tower like giants before me,
Casting glittering shadows into the placid lakes at their feet
Burnished orange hills stand behind me,
Like minuscule versions of the giants in front.
The tranquil waters of the lakes at the mountain feet,
Have not even a ripple to mar their beauty.
Everything is so still, calm and serene
A cool, gentle breeze soothes me,
And carries all my troubles away
I feel safe,
Like the mountains are protecting me from danger
Maybe it's not so bad to be lost!

Emma Collins (14)
Coleraine High School

ORANGE

The fluorescent orange fruit
Bright and very visible,
Feels like pimples crawling up your arms.
Sweet when ripe like a bright sun
It never makes a noise,
As silent as a mouse
Except when eaten
A squishy, squashy noise
A very refreshing fruit,
Like being on a tropical island.

Elizabeth Crowe (13)
Coleraine High School

STARS

Twinkling, dazzling,
Bright and gleaming
The stars sit happy in the sky.
Surrounded by a sea of darkness.
They twinkle like little diamonds
And as I watch them from down below;
I can see them form shapes and smile and glow.
Suddenly one moves as quick as lightning,
Disappearing like angel dust.
Never to be seen again;
Gone without a trace,
And the only thing left are a few friends
That fill in its space.

Carli Connor (13)
Coleraine High School

THE SKY

Some say that the sky holds another world,
A magical world where you can live in peace,
Where the birds are your closest friends,
And you hope that this peace will never end,
When you are young you lie and think,
Would those clouds be soft and fluffy
You wish you could fly up to the sky,
And when you do you will lie on those soft clouds,
Nobody knows what the sky will bring,
Sun, rain, wind or snow it's just a guess,
When it is raining you have to stay inside,
And when it is sunny you go outside and play about.

Alison Archer (13)
Coleraine High School

THE APPLE

It is smooth and round like the Earth.
Short and stubby.
Glistening green like a meadow filled with luscious grass.
Delicious with a golden shine.
When bitten the flavours fill your mouth,
Like a waterfall gushing into a lake
The sound is like the cracking of a wooden stick in two.
The slight bruises bend the shape and build the character.
The stalk bent to one side,
Occasionally with a leaf,
Sticks out from the centre of the apple commonly known as the core,
Which in turn runs through the middle of the fruit like a steel pole,
Keeping it up
This is left when the rest has gone.

Sharon Hoy (13)
Coleraine High School

WINTER

She lies in the snow with only a newspaper,
Shivering from the cold, shivering from the rain
As darkness falls the rain appears,
And the raindrops cling to her defenceless body.
She awakens to the trickling of the rain,
And quickens her pace as the winds swirl,
And runs as the dark, grey clouds seep in.
As the wind howls and the rain runs,
She tightens her jacket to keep herself warm;
It's just her, the rain and her newspaper.

Lesley-Anne Peters (13)
Coleraine High School

PLUM

Sitting there,
Tempting me,
With all its elegance.
Its colour, like something out of space,
A dark maroon sweeps its face,
With a tint of red, like a ruby, a jewel,
And through it glides a misty blue.
I'm afraid,
Afraid I can't resist its shininess,
And the heart shape,
That appears at only one angle.
I reach further pulling it towards me, like an asteroid,
Spinning, turning,
Too late.
Doomsday . . .
It has reached my lips,
I bite.
The hard sour skin peels like ribbon.
It leaves a tinge of sourness in my mouth,
But below it there is gold.
A peach, orange under skin has met my gaze.
As I go further under it's outer shell, I begin to slow.
What's stopping me?
A hard wicked stone peeps out at me.
I tear all the juicy flesh away and I'm left with nothing,
Nothing but a hideous purple centre,
The centre of the once beautiful, glorious fruit.
The rest, well it's in
Oblivion.

Rachael Vauls (13)
Coleraine High School

A Tortoise's Head

Inside,
There is a gear stick,
Which goes from one mile per hour to ten.

Crunch, crunch,
Munch, munch,
A green leaf,
Sounds nice.

Worries about everything,
For example
Have I still got my protective shell?
Or
Do I smell?

Am I still a lady-killer?
Or
Have I lost my touch!
I wonder does Miss Tortoise like me very much!

Sleep, sleep,
Zzzz, Zzzz,
Sleeping,
Sounds nice.

Isn't life too short?
I think I'll take it slow,
Just like my great, great Uncle Joe!

Alison Cameron (13)
Coleraine High School

In The Future

I would like to go into space one day,
Planets, stars and sun.
I'd like one day to do something,
No one's already done.
I'd like to build a building,
One thousand storeys tall
Then do an enormous bungee jump
Down the building's wall.
I'd like to dive under water
Lower than ever before
And I'll make sure that my life,
Certainly isn't a bore.
I'd like to make a pizza
That no one could ever eat,
Because it's bigger
Than Finn McCool's feet.
I'd like to write a poem
That's not extremely long,
I'd call it 'In The Future'
The name can't go wrong.
I'd like to write a film
As good as 'Pitch Black'
(Have you ever seen that one?
There's nothing good it lacks.)
I'll invent a machine
A dream-recorder machine.
You'd get up in the morning
And relive your dream.
In conclusion, I'd like to say
I will do all these some day.

Naomi Moore (12)
Coleraine High School

A Spring Morning

Calmness covers the countryside,
On this young spring morning
Trees sit delicately on the untouched dew,
With their arms spread,
Flaunting their newly grown suits
Of sweet-smelling floret
They watch over the emerald fields,
Gazing at the crisp grass
And the dew,
Sitting prettily upon every strand
Like a shimmering drop of crystal
The contour of the countryside
Meets the azure sky, lonely
Without a cloud, but still
It listens to the wind
Rushing through the trees,
Carelessly pulling off blossom.
Each petal falls quietly into the jade sea,
Its looks untroubled and happy
But suddenly a noise breaks the silence,
A church bell rings forcefully,
The sound of people chattering
The countryside now knows,
A spring morning has just woken up.

Victoria Harbinson (14)
Coleraine High School

A Moment In Time

A moment in time . . . where I laugh, where I cry,
Where I enjoy my life.

Up and down I might go,
Round and round I go . . . I love my life, it is fun.

Season to season my life rolls on and on,
I enjoy it all.
From spring to autumn, playing sport and swimming.

Oh how I love my life . . . *this* moment in time!

Christena Moore (14)
Limegrove School

MOTORBIKE

M uggers steal people's handbags,
O pen the bags and take the money,
T ake any credit cards,
O nly the police can help
R ing 999 and the police will come to help
B ikes are fast and can chase the mugger
I nto their houses,
K eeping people safe
E vil muggers arrested.

William O'Hara (12)
Limegrove School

RIOT GEAR

R ing the police if you are in trouble,
I f you are in trouble ring - nine, nine, nine.
O fficers always protect the police station
T errorists are bad.

G roups of police go to football matches,
E very policeman protects people.
A rrest terrorists
R ioters need to be stopped.

Scott McElwee (12)
Limegrove School

SOMEONE SPECIAL

There is this boy I know,
He makes my heart and blood flow.

Every time I see him my heart beats faster and faster,
My love for him will last and last.

No one knows how much he means to me
In fast I wish he and I could be close forever.

My love for him in my heart will never stop,
It is like doves and swallows.

I hope my heart stays close to his heart,
No one will ever keep us apart
Because he will always be in my heart.

Shona McCloskey (13)
Limegrove School

INVESTIGATE

I   llegal drugs taken away,
N   ever ever drink and drive,
V   iolent people arrested,
E   mergencies investigated,
S   afe children from bad people,
T   hieves stealing things,
I   nvestigating all crimes!
G   angs put in jail,
A   rrest robbers,
T   eams working together,
E   nd crime!

Matthew Crawford (12)
Limegrove School

EMOTIONS

H   is for high spirits
A   is for adoration
L   is for love
L   is for laughter
O   is for obedience
W   is for wickedness
E   is for elation
E   is for enjoyment
N   is for naughtiness

N   is for naivety
I   is for innocence
G   is for gaiety
H   is for happiness
T   is for temper

Ryan Johnston (13)
Magherafelt High School

IN THE PLAYGROUND

Chasing, racing,
Munching, crunching,
Moaning, groaning,
Fighting, biting,
Splashing, dashing,
Thumping, jumping,
Calling, falling,
Talking, walking
    and off goes the bell and
    slowly we make our way
    to our next class.

Leanne Nesbitt (13)
Magherafelt High School

THE LION

In the midst of Africa,
Lives a predacious beast
That hunts and kills animals
Which it then eats for a feast.

The lion stalks with its pride,
In the long savannah grass,
Harassing its prey
Which it will devour so fast.

The lion's mane flashes brightly in the sun
As along the ground it quietly creeps
Its claws and teeth ready to kill
As it takes one final leap.

Pouncing silently on its unsuspecting prey
You can only hear a muffled squeal
As claws tear into the bloody flesh
And the lion settles to enjoy its meal.

Philip Crossett (12)
Magherafelt High School

TRAGEDY IN AMERICA

One day some men hijacked a plane
Threatening people with knives.
They changed the destination to New York
And headed for the World Trade Centre.

People looked up in amazement
As they saw the plane crash.
They were all stunned at the crash
When another plane crashed.

The two buildings started to collapse
As people ran for their lives.
Fire fighters looked for more survivors
But their chances of finding anyone were slim.

Alan Jones (13)
Magherafelt High School

MY GRANDA

My *granda* is the type of man
Who likes to fix and mend
All kinds of gadgets new and old
And sell them to his friends.

My g*randa* is the type of man
Who likes to drive his cars,
MGs and vintage tractors,
To rallies near and far.

My g*randa* is the type of man
Who likes to go to shoot
Clay birds, pheasants and odd Mallard Duck,
But now he prefers to cook.

My g*randa* is the type of man
Who likes an antique fair,
Old clocks, old lamps, old bric-a-brac,
You'll find him plundering there.

My g*randa* is the type of man
Whom I am learning from,
To work, to play, to have some fun
And get the job well done,
He'll always be the one,
My granda.

Christopher Morrow (13)
Magherafelt High School

WHAT'S THAT IN THE BUSH

One day I was walking down the street,
I said, 'That bush just squeaked!'
It was some men covered in oil leaks,
And out of the bushes they did peek.

They were in the bushes and in the trees,
They weren't standing but on their knees.
Whatever they were wearing they got fleas,
Even other insects such as bees.

The men were covered in brown and green,
Nobody knows where else they've been.
For some reason they were very keen,
One of them called out the name Dean.

I went home and asked my mum,
She told me why they had to come.
'Now go and sit down my son.'
I looked for a seat but there were none!

She said, 'It's camouflage my son!'

June Speers (12)
Magherafelt High School

MY PET HAMSTER

I have a pet hamster called Stuart
He's so small and fat
He has small ears and a small tail
But really big teeth.

In his cage he runs round his wheel
Up and down the pipes he goes
But when he's sleeping
You just better not wake him.

He loves out of his cage
To run around the floor
He loves hiding in the corners
But doesn't like going back into his cage again.

William Davison (14)
Magherafelt High School

A FEW WOMEN AND THEIR DOGS

There once were three ladies with dogs,
They loved their doggies so much.
Every week they would try to train,
To go in the house and not touch.

And now one of the women called Flo,
Took her black dog to the show.
She knew that Smut was the best,
And would easily outclass the rest.

Now Ivy loved her wee puppy,
She taught it to do lots of tricks.
Wuffles could fetch her slippers,
And would cover her face in licks.

The third and last little lady,
Let her dog run wildly around.
Then one day that rascal Bailey,
Pushed her down to the ground.

Now these women are older,
And their doggies all have died.
And because they loved their wee doggies,
They got new ones, Fudge, Sally and Tide.

Andie Purvis (13)
Magherafelt High School

TERROR IN AMERICA!

On the 11th of September in America,
It was just a normal day,
People out working, shopping, enjoying themselves,
But not for much longer.

Suddenly two planes crashed into the twin towers,
People were in shock, crying, didn't know what to do,
People were dead, and some looking
For their loved ones.

Other people were trying to escape,
Fire-fighters, police coming to save lives,
Lots of people were scared of dying,
Some calm, knowing they would live.

Suddenly another crash, but this time,
Into the Pentagon.
What was happening
Who was doing this to America,
And why?

The 11th of September was a shock to us all,
Why would anyone do this to us?
Tell me why, who was it?
Whoever did this will regret it because,

United States of America
Will fight back!

Charlene Gilmore (13)
Magherafelt High School

HALLOWE'EN

Hallowe'en is the one night
When you get the biggest scare,
You can't travel alone
But then you wouldn't dare!

It's the one night when I believe in superstitions
Such as ghouls, Frankenstein and witches,
It's the one night when all this comes true
So keep a close eye behind you.

So if you wander into a castle
Remember Dracula and Frankenstein,
To them you're a hassle
So don't stay to dine!

But we can't forget Jool the Ghoul
For that would be a sin,
If you go near and touch him, you would be a fool
For in this battle you'd definitely not win.

Then there's Wiona Witch
Who lives in a cave,
Who makes spells in cauldrons
And keeps a skeleton as a slave.

So when it comes Hallowe'en
You're sure to get a fright,
For witches and ghouls
And fools like you travel alone that night!

Emma Charlene Campbell (12)
Magherafelt High School

AUTUMN TURNS TO WINTER

Autumn is here once again
With winds and lots of heavy rain.

Trees and leaves are changing colour
Golden brown, not green as in summer.

Our clothes are warmer to beat the chill
Children are excited with the Hallowe'en thrill.

As time goes back and nights get darker
We feel the cold winds get even sharper.

Soon harvest is over and next is Christmas
Warm fires glow and the windows are misted.

Each year it seems to be the same things
But in everyone's lives, changes they bring.

Time stands still for no man they say
And times goes on day by day.

Andrew Stewart (13)
Magherafelt High School

JUDY

My little Judy is a dote,
She loves it when I sing a note,
She barks with joy and delight,
Especially late at night!

We take her for a walk at night,
She likes to run and have some fun,
The grass is soft,
The road is hard,
But this does not stop Judy from running hard.

She likes to sleep when she comes home,
But how her ears rise up when dad says, 'Let's go.'
We understand why she goes slow,
As she cannot turn round and say, 'No!'

Kelly McKee (13)
Magherafelt High School

CRUISING

It's almost dark
A snake in the park
It's red, it's blue
It's silver too.

The snake is moving
It's fast, it's slow
It's long, it's short
From head to toe.

We join in
Just for a spin
It's for a lark
Before we park.

The snake has stopped
And out we drop
For up ahead
There is a cop.

So home we go
Now driving slow
We will return
To take our turn.

Michael Hutchinson (13)
Magherafelt High School

THE SEASONS

Spring will bring all the flowers
And make our days have longer hours.
Then young chicks will appear
As soon as spring is near.

Summer's long, hot, lazy days
Lots of cool drinks mum says.
Leaves rustle on all the trees
I'll lie under them to get a breeze.

Autumn brings a stronger breeze
And all the leaves come off the trees.
Rain comes to stay
Until the end of the day.

Winter is here and I'm full of cheer
Christmas is my favourite time of year.
Presents galore under the tree
That's where you will find me.

Aaron Purvis (13)
Magherafelt High School

HORSES

Horses here
Horses there
Horses everywhere.

Some fast
Some slow
Some coloured
Others white as snow.

Horses big
Horses small
Ploughing, sowing, carting
Useful for all jobs.

Sleek and fast
Slow and showy
Graceful in their stride
Strength and elegance as one.

Richard Davis (13)
Magherafelt High School

MY NIECE

My niece she is a perfect child
Oh dear me
Her mother is my sister
One asks how could that be?

She eats the plants
She eats the soil
She's always on the prowl
And when she's really, really bad
You can hear her granda howl.

She is lovely, she is beautiful
She's full of joy and glee
She gets off with 'blue murder'
Because she's only three.

She is pretty, she is wonderful
She's really, really clever
She loves her gran, but most of all
She loves her clever uncle!

Sam Lee (13)
Magherafelt High School

THE EXCUSE

Out from behind a corner,
Jumped a big black dog,
It snatched the paper from me
And ran off down the road.

I ran down the road after it,
But soon I was out of breath,
And I had to stop to have a rest.

It was just for a second, sir
I looked a different way,
And when I looked around again,
The dog had gone away.

I looked for ages for it, sir
But it had disappeared,
And then I came to tell you,
Why my homework isn't here.

Andrea Henderson (13)
Magherafelt High School

ANGER

Anger is bright *red.*
It tastes like *blood.*
It smells like *red-hot fire.*
It looks like a *bonfire.*
It sounds like a *bomb* going off.
And it feels like all of these put
Together!

William Brown (12)
Magherafelt High School

One After Another

One step after another and
the longest walk is ended.
One stitch after another an
the widest hole is mended.
One brick upon another and
the highest wall is made.
One flake upon another and
the deepest snow is laid.
One penny upon another and
the pounds will soon mount up.
One lodgement after another and
the interest comes on top.
One class after another and
school days are soon past.
One year after another and
it's pension time, at last.
One smile after another and
life's one sunny ray,
Turning a gloomy person's life
into a sunny day.

Claire Moore (12)
Magherafelt High School

Kiwi

Kiwi
Green and oval
Furry and rough
Tingly on my tongue
Bitter to eat!

Hanna Lawrence (13)
Magherafelt High School

The Dreaded Teacher!

There I was, ready to go in,
Then he shouted, 'That's enough fun.
Boys go first, girls go last
Sit down quick and make it fast.

Get out your books, work begins now
Write this down, or there's be a huge row.'
'But sir, this is boring, can't we do something else?'
'Of course you cannot, so get back to your work.

Because of your remark, you have just earned yourself detention,
Which you may not like.
So get on your bike and take a hike
And don't open your mouth again this night.

You've got yourself school rules, detention
And also you are suspended.
You are lucky that it has stopped there
Or else you could have been expelled.'

Lisa Bowman (12)
Magherafelt High School

School

I don't like school
Other people think it's cool.
Teachers dishing out school rules
'Cause we're all acting like fools.

Teachers sometimes are a pain
Homework is the name of the game.
If homework is handed in late
I know I'll soon be in a state.

Getting up in the morning is a drag
And having to pack our heavy school bag.
Heavy text books and files,
Walking to school which seems like miles.

Claire Wallace (12)
Magherafelt High School

THE SEASONS

It does come in the autumn of the years
Daylight is shorter and darkness appears
Leaves, harvesting, whistling of the winds
Autumn finishes and winter begins

Wet and dank the days are black
Everyone is morbid, sombre and depressed
But there hails Christmas with festive joy and meetings
Makes life worthwhile with Good Will and Season's Greetings

Now the spring of year is near to hand
Snowdrops and daffodils cover the land
Ploughing the fields and sowing the crops
Those hardworking farmers never stop

But we need sunshine in summer to brighten our days
Children and family outings being arranged
Seaside, beaches, buckets and spades
Glorious holidays are happily being made

For all the seasons of the year are needed
Autumn, winter, spring and summer included
Climates, time changes for many reasons
This is what we call the *seasons*

Gyles McAllen (12)
Magherafelt High School

WINTER

I love the wintertime.
The sound of the church bell chime.
The blanket of snow, it's so bright and white.
Children out making snowmen,
And having snowball fights.

I love the wintertime.
The sound of the wind howling outside,
And us snuggled up in our warm beds inside.
The days get shorter.
The nights get longer.

I love the wintertime.
We get loads of presents at Christmas.
But this isn't the main reason for Christmas.
It is that Jesus was born in a manger
And He and His parents had to flee from danger.

Ruth Linton (12)
Magherafelt High School

OPERATION

O pen heart surgery.
P lease help nurse.
E lephant or butterfly?
R ough, no we do not let it hurt.
A fter the recovery room you will get better.
T he nurses will look after you.
I   will be doing your
O peration.
N ow you will feel better.

James Dempsey (12)
Magherafelt High School

WIND

Winter winds roar about
to be heard we have to shout.

Blowing at the windowpane
making all the trees strain.

Howling at us through the night
whistling with all its might.

Draughts are coming under the door
lifting the mat from the floor.

Gales are ruining all the flowers
but scarves protect us from its powers.

It blows the apples from the trees
leaving nothing but the leaves.

Claire Fullerton (12)
Magherafelt High School

REAL COOL

We're real cool,
Thought we'd leave school,

We stayed out late,
Played with our mates,

We played with sin,
Bought gin,

We died soon,

But we thought we were cool,
All we were was fools.

Sharon Montgomery (12)
Magherafelt High School

SHOW JUMPING

Horse and rider,
Two as one
Jump the fences one by one.
With awesome turns
And clicking hooves,
Combining skills with
Natural moves.

Horse and rider,
Trust to trust,
To win the cup is a must.
Lap of honour,
Simply the best,
Roaring crowds,
So *very, very, very* proud.

Laura Brown (12)
Magherafelt High School

THE GNU

There once was a gnu
Who was new to the zoo
He asked another gnu
What he should do
The other gnu said
Shaking his head
'If I knew
I would have told you
I'm
New
Too!'

Gareth Booth (11)
Magherafelt High School

CANDYFLOSS

I'm pink or blue
And tasty too!
I'm quite puffy
And really fluffy.

I'm sugary and sweet
And a big treat,
I taste like strawberry
Or even raspberry.

I'm on a stick
And I'm nice to lick,
But it doesn't matter if you're on a diet
Just go out and buy it!

So if you really want a treat
Buy me, I'm not that sweet,
Enjoy me as I melt in your mouth
I'm just a great big candyfloss.

Lee-Anne Duncan (12)
Magherafelt High School

WAR

There is war, war all around
In the air
And on the ground
Tanks are roaring, sirens sound
Thousands of dead men can be found
Jets are flying, men are dying
Mothers are crying
And nations are sighing.

Matthew Gallick (11)
Magherafelt High School

OH THE RAIN IS SO ANNOYING

Oh the rain is so annoying.
It's there in the morning.
It's there when I go to school,
And when I come home.
Oh the rain is so annoying.

Oh the rain is so annoying.
It's there when I watch TV,
On Emmerdale, the weather and ITV.
Oh the rain is so annoying.

Oh the rain is so annoying.
It's there all year round,
When we want it and when we don't.
Oh the rain is so annoying.

Oh the rain is so annoying.
It makes puddles
And muddy patches.
It makes our clothes wet and our hair not sit.
Oh the rain is so annoying.

Cathy Gilmour (13)
Magherafelt High School

MY CAT PATCH

My cat Patch is lazy
She will lick herself all day,
In her basket purring
Sleeping snug deep in the hay.

In the morning sunshine she will come and play
With her little kittens skipping along the way,
Tumbling, chasing, leaping, enjoying the fun
Until the sun goes down and they are all done.

Patch is in the meadow watching for her prey
She will sit there quietly, even all day,
Then quickly, silently, leaping with a bounce
She will get her prey with one big pounce!

Emma Palmer (11)
Magherafelt High School

FOOTBALL, FOOTBALL

Football, football it's so good
Past the line if you could
If you do, what a goal
Sorry Goalie, it's not your day

Football, football it's so good
So much sweat, don't want to use
So many tackles to be done
So many injuries to worry about

Football, football it's so good
Up late at night and up so early
Some good stations, some hard teams
This is the night for some team's dreams

Football, football it's so good
It's so tiring, let's go home
What a save, what a miss
Oh what a bad tackle

Football, football it's so good
It's the night for the champions
It's a penalty, what a goal!
Good cross, but no one at the end

Ian Brown (11)
Magherafelt High School

HALLOWE'EN

Hallowe'en night is now here
All the adults are going mad
Laughter is in the air
Lights are in the sky
Old houses give me the creeps
Witches are on the prowl
Eight shots going all around
Everybody is playing with a sparkler
Nights are darker and longer now

Never go out on your own
In every house children play
Give each friend an apple please
Hallowe'en is nearly over
Time to go to bed, it's safe there.

Robert Glendinning (12)
Magherafelt High School

BEDTIME

The night is dark
Black and gloom
With all good luck
You'll fall asleep soon
If you don't
You're in trouble
The noises make you scared
Make you snuggle
The bogey man is about
If you get scared he makes you shout
So turn on the light to look for him
Under the bed or above your head.

James Higgins (13)
Magherafelt High School

MY DOG

Me and my dog go out to play
Until it gets to the end of the day
Then it's time to go in, to our beds to sleep.

When the next day comes we then get up to play
Then we walk to school together
And I count the minutes until home time.

At three o'clock I run out of the room
Up the street to see my dog Spike
And then we go out to the park to play.

When I go in to do my homework
He lies and watches at me feet
And then I give him his dinner which he loves so much.

Me and my dog are friends forever.

Pamela Davis (11)
Magherafelt High School

RULES

Work hard or get in trouble.
Rules, rules they're all a muddle.
Rules should be only for a mess.
Instead they're just a pest.
Come to school at any time.
After all it's not a crime.
Classes, classes they are so long.
We should learn about Hong Kong.
Wear make-up and high shoes.
Rules, rules they're the latest news.

Nicola Jordan (13)
Magherafelt High School

SPRINGTIME

I love to see the springtime
And hear the birdies sing.
The dawn chorus in the morning
Is my delight to hear.

The flowers are also glowing
With the early morning sunshine
And the little lambs are
Skipping round the meadow so green.

Listen! I hear old Rover barking
As the farmer comes up the lane.
Rover hunts away the rabbit
That is hiding under the tree.

The grass is wet with the early morning dew
And the cattle are content upon the hill.
The farmer whistles a merry tune
Everyone so joyful, spring is here again.

Emma Forde (11)
Magherafelt High School

MY BROTHER

My brother is a pain,
He always calls me names,
If I call him some names,
He always beats me up!

My brother is not wise,
He's got a real junk car,
He always drives it fast
And doesn't really care.

Sometimes he is loveable,
And sometimes maybe not,
Sometimes he's a bad boy,
And sometimes he is good.

My brother is a funny boy,
He always plays some jokes,
Sometimes they are scary,
And sometimes maybe not.

Zara Morrison (11)
Magherafelt High School

SISTERS, SISTERS, SUCH A PAIN

Sisters, sisters, such a pain
they are always right
and not to blame.

Sisters, sisters, such a pain
whoever wants a sister
must be insane.

Sisters, sisters, such a pain
they are always cheeky
and always in a daze.

Sisters, sisters, such a pain
they think they are smart
but think again.

Sisters, sisters, such a pain
now I am fed up
so why don't I
send her off in an aeroplane.

Sharon Ferguson (12)
Magherafelt High School

MY TWO BROTHERS

My two brothers are really caring
They are sometimes helpful, sometimes not,
Some brothers are rude, kind or funny
But my two brothers are great.

Calling names of course is their main hobby
Just for attention,
I know they are just fooling around
Different brothers they just like to be.

One is very helpful in the house, the other an outdoor boy
Christmas, birthdays they never forget,
All the useful things I get
Show how much they really think of me.

People think sisters don't care
Sometimes true, sometimes not,
I worry that they're okay
I'm sure they just do the same about me.

Be grateful for those brothers
For when trouble comes
You know they are only a shout away,
That's why they mean so much to me.

Leanne Davison (11)
Magherafelt High School

ANIMALS

Black and white, green and brown,
And colours oh so bright,
Some are seen in morning sun,
And some in the dark of night.
Ones who bark and howl and roar,
And ones so silent run to hide underground,
As a farmer runs to get his gun.

The best of all God's creatures,
Are the pets we have at home,
'Cos we can lift and cuddle them,
And they never seem to roam.
What would our world be today,
If animals decided not to stay?

Samantha Finlay (11)
Magherafelt High School

SUMMER!

Summer is great,
Summer is fun,
It won't be fun,
If there's no sun.

I like to go to the seaside,
And make sand castles with my buckets,
I like to jump the waves,
Close to the tide.

I bring my bodyboard,
Hoping there will be good waves,
The waves are as rough as a sword,
And once I saw some caves.

I love going abroad,
And hopefully get tanned,
I love joining the kids' club,
But I hate getting banned.

When I go abroad,
I love jumping in the pool,
And splashing my sisters,
I love the pool, cos it's cool!

Laura Jamison (13)
Magherafelt High School

PETS

Pets, pets, what a pain
whoever wants one is insane.

Pets, pets, drive you mad
barking and purring all day long.

People think it so great
to have a pet around,
something to be proud of
but just for a little while.

But pets can be so loveable
to have around
to keep you company
whenever you are down.

Keeping pets is such a hard job
but after all, it's well worth it.

Stacey Hassan (11)
Magherafelt High School

A NOISY NIGHT

Noisy neighbours in the street
Shouting at me as I peep
Singing lads, kicking cans
Oh to catch those drinking fans.

Girls and lads, screaming out
'Burn some rubber,' they do shout
Oh for peace so I can sleep
Then I wouldn't have to peep.

Kicking bins, knocking doors
Oh how my head is sore
Oh the sound of breaking glass
All because of that old bass.

'Go away,' I cannot shout
For fear they put me out
So I lie awake, a young lass
All because of that old bass.

Julie Gregg (12)
Magherafelt High School

MY DREAM CAR

There are many ways to travel,
But the best by far,
Is to travel with me in my dream car.

With the power of a jet,
The two bright sparkling exhausts
Blow out rings of fury,
As I drive off at great speed.

Four low profile tyres
Squeak and squeal,
As the brakes are applied
As I approach a red light.

I tingle with excitement
As I zoom off once more,
Like a shooting star
In my super dream car.

David Barfoot (12)
Magherafelt High School

YOU'RE LATE

'You're late, what have you to say?'
'Well Miss, I couldney find ma glasses
And I couldney see me uniform.
And then me granda fell doon the stairs
And I had tay get him sorted.
Then I lost me Billy snake behind the kitchen chair
And I really missed him Miss!
Then me wheel fell off me bike and I had tay get it fixed.'
'You missed form class and first period.'
'But I'm sorry, it wasney my fault.'
'I don't care, if it was or wasney your fault
You have got break, dinner and after school detention.
You have just told me a lot of excuses and rubbish.
I am very disappointed with you.

*Now off you go and don't be late
And make up no more excuses.'*

Stacey Boone (11)
Magherafelt High School

THE DAY THE WORLD SHOOK

It was on TV
For the world to see
The day thousands died
The two planes crashed without any bother
Into the towers beside each other
The first tower crumbled, the second followed
While the millions that watched took a breath and swallowed
Sorrow and grief and disbelief
Was the day the world shook.

William Henderson (14)
Magherafelt High School

HOME

Home is a place where I feel safe
Home is a place where I have faith,
Home is a place where Dad has the power
To send me to a warm shower.

Kitchen is a place where I can cook
Kitchen is a place where I can read a book,
Kitchen is a place where I can eat my tea
Kitchen is a place where we like to be.

Bedroom is a place where I can sleep
Bedroom is a place where I can weep,
Bedroom is a place where I can eat and drink
Bedroom is a place where I can think.

Home is a place where Mum and Dad say,
'Get to your bed,' at the end of the day.

Thomas Shannon (11)
Magherafelt High School

AMERICA IN TEARS!

On the 11th of September 2001,
the world's worst terrorist incident had just begun.
The suicide bombers they hijacked four planes
They crashed without mercy, what had they to gain?
They demolished the Twin Towers,
The Pentagon too!
Thousands were killed, there was nothing they could do,
Families are heartbroken, while they search for their dead
At the place where some of the bodies were laid
America has promised to get its revenge,
To wipe out the terrorists - will things ever change?

Matthew Hyndman (11)
Magherafelt High School

HALLOWE'EN

H allowe'en night is here once again
A ll the children play their games
L ots of fireworks begin to fly
L ighting up the night sky
O range pumpkins with faces shine
W itches on broomsticks fly in line
E erie noises all around
E eks and squeaks and spooky sounds
N oisy bangers and sparklers too.

N ot too near the animals, shh!
I n the night of fun and fright
G hosts and goblins are in flight
H aving fun in fancy dress
T rick or treat is the best.

Andrew Derby (11)
Magherafelt High School

SCHOOL

S ports that I love to do.
C lever children come to learn.
H olidays we all look forward to.
O oh can't forget about detention which nobody likes unless
they're mad.
O rdinary pupils . . . even the teachers.
L ying boys and girls who make up excuses because they forgot to do
their homework.

Gary Jordan (13)
Magherafelt High School

FOOTBALL

Football, football it is really great
Football, football when they're playing a team I hate.
Football, football it is really fun
Football, football when you see them run.

Football, football it is really great
Football, football it's not when you're late.
Football, football it's football galore
Football, football it's good when they score.

Hack, dribble, shoot, and score
As well as that there's plenty more.
Like free-kicks, penalties, yellow cards,
Corners, that's what makes football brilliant.

Alan McClean (11)
Magherafelt High School

MUSIC

Music is like a pleasure trip,
lifting you from the gloom
of this old world with tears and fears,
transporting you to the moon.

To some, music is but a drag
to me it's so much more,
the rock, the pop, the jazz, the rap
it makes me want to soar.

Music is like a first class meal
with all the right ingredients,
The sound of harp, violin and piano,
they soothe like a tranquil river.

Paul Somerville (11)
Magherafelt High School

FIREWORKS

Hundreds of fireworks
Big and small,
Lots of colours
Watch them fall.
Light the sparklers
Listen to the fizzle,
Drop them in a puddle
Hear them sizzle.
Every year it's the same
Now, let's get to the games.

First we meet
For trick or treat,
We rap doors
And then retreat.
Duck for apples
In a basin,
The fire's lit
Our hearts are racing.

This night is full
Of fun and fear,
Why does it come
Just once a year?
As dawn arrives
With a glow,
All night creatures
Return below!

Raymond Bigger (11)
Magherafelt High School

HALLOWE'EN

The darkness has fallen, the vampires are here
It's Hallowe'en the scary time of year.

With spooky faces and long wooden brooms
The witches are out and around they zoom!

Don't try to run, don't try to hide
The devil will catch you and then you'll be fried.

The banging and crashing
And then all the flashing.

The eating of nuts
And the chewing of guts.

The eating of cats
By witches in hats.

Getting near dawn
The vampires have gone.

Hope you were listening
'Cause next year you could be sizzling!

David Michael (11)
Magherafelt High School

SADNESS

Sadness is a dark! Dark! Colour
It tastes like cold lumpy pudding
It smells out of this world
Sadness looks like my homework when my dog has eaten it
It sounds like long sharp nails running down a blackboard
It feels like slime running down your back.

Malcolm Watterson (12)
Magherafelt High School

MY CAT

His name is Tigger and he has orange stripes.
My cat is always miaowing in the morning looking for food.
Every time the phone rings he miaows into it to say hello.
At Christmas time he goes crazy at the tree trying to knock the
        baubles off.
He always wants to say hello by brushing around my legs.
My granda does not like cats and Tigger purrs around him all the time.
Scratching on my mum's carpet with his claws makes her really cross.
In the autumn time he likes to chase the leaves falling off the trees.
He has his favourite chair to curl up in and sleep.
In the dark his eyes light up and scare me.
When we come home Tigger always appears to say hello.
Most of all I love my cat because he curls up in bed beside me.

Richard McFadden (11)
Magherafelt High School

HALLOWE'EN

Hallowe'en is a great time of year,
When scary costumes and masks appear,
With fireworks crackling and banging
Screaming and whizzing,
Around in circles
When beautiful colours go high up in the sky.
Trick or treating, knocking on people's door.
When the night comes to an end
Small children with bags of candy
Get into bed for a nice rest
After running about the street at night
Remembering all the fun they had.
Trick or treat night wasn't so bad.

Gemma Mawhinney (13)
Magherafelt High School

SPAGHETTI

A plate full of spaghetti,
All covered in hot tomato sauce,
It's my favourite meal,
It just looks like

Twisted
    Wound
Up
    Worms!

I like lifting them up and swallowing them very quickly.
After wriggling them down my throat,
I finish and go and look at myself in the bathroom mirror.

I notice that my shirt is covered in tomato ketchup
And it makes me think that I need a baby's bib.

Cherith Scott (12)
Magherafelt High School

MAN UNITED

Man United, what a wonderful team,
With Barthez and Beckham,
And Veron, van Nistelrooy and not forgetting
The last minute sub Solskjaer
Who scored to make it 2-1
And United finally became the Champions of Europe again.

Nobody can stop this awesome team,
Who on their way to win the premiership beat
Aston Villa, Leeds, Arsenal, the list is endless
So just remember United are the best!

Stephen Simpson (13)
Magherafelt High School

HALLOWE'EN

Hallowe'en is coming near
The witches putting us all in fear
Whistling through the moonlight air
Laughing and tossing their long black hair.

The children love to play trick or treat
Hoping for nuts or perhaps some sweets
They duck for apples and jump for joy
The girls might also be looking for a boy!

Boys and girls might want to play chase
Showing off their glowing, painted face
Fireworks go off with a bang and a crack
Sparkling bright colours and then it's black.

Stories are told of ghosts from the dead
With vampires sucking the blood so red
The autumn leaves rustle and I hear an owl hoot
I'm really scared something's creeping on my foot!

Richard Love (11)
Magherafelt High School

LOVE!

Love is pink and nice,
Love is lovely and sweet like spice!
Love smells quite nice!

Love is like one hundred silver flutes
Playing your favourite song.
Love feels like heaven!

Janice Watterson (13)
Magherafelt High School

MY MUM

My mum is always there,
When times are tough,
When I have a problem,
When I need a hand,
Always there to wake me up,
But most of all when I need a hug.

My mum and I do lots together,
Cooking, cleaning, walking and talking.
My mum and I sometimes fight,
But always make up.
My mum calls me 'her angel'
I call her 'my number one'.

I sometimes wonder if I will turn out like her.
I hope I will.
My mum is the best and I wouldn't swap her
For all the money in China.

Eleanor Averill (14)
Magherafelt High School

FOOTBALL

Sliding, falling
Winning, losing
Scoring, missing
Running, kicking
Tackling, saving
Conceding, beating
Defending, attacking
Being the best you can be

Alan Kennedy (13)
Magherafelt High School

HALLOWE'EN FRIGHTS

Hallowe'en is near
And we are all in fear.

Witches are flying with their black hats
And so are the vampire bats.

Cats which are black
Are caught in witch's sacks.

The place is crawling with mice
Which are not one bit nice.

Cats are after the rats
Which are hiding under your doormats.

Fireworks are in the air
That's a tenner away if you dare!

Bangers are being sold
Only buy them if you are bold.

Vampires are flying but only at night
Watch they don't give you an awful fright!

Philip Dickson (11)
Magherafelt High School

JOY

Joy is a heart-warming red
The taste is like a strawberry bed
The smell is like a freshly baked pudding pie
It looks like a summer's day spell
It sounds happy and glad
It feels like a cosy lie in bed.

Nial Fleming (12)
Magherafelt High School

ANIMALS

A stripey kitten sitting on the wall:
Look at how small it is
Let's go to the pet shop to see what we can see
Mum said we could have a pet
We jumped with glee
My sister and me
We were very excited.

We picked a parrot
It was so colourful and bright colour
It was a wonderful sight
We looked at rabbits
They were eating carrots
We looked at hamsters, mice and all things nice.

We told the man which one we would like
We pointed at the parrot.
'What a fine bird you have picked.'
'Thank you.'
'What is its name?' we asked.
'Rainbow,' the man said.

Melissa Carole Purvis (11)
Magherafelt High School

HAPPINESS

Happiness is the sound of laughter.
It tastes like strawberries.
Happiness looks like the sun,
Shining on a warm day.
Happiness is like flowers in the wind.
Happiness is bright and breezy.

Rebecca McGrath (12)
Magherafelt High School

FIREWORKS

Fireworks bright and light,
flying through the night.
Bursting into colours
in the pale moonlight.
Lighting up the sky
as if it was alive.
Looks like fireflies flying
through the air.
Loud and soft like missiles
exploding in the sky.
Like spaceships on a mission to space
down to hit the ground.
Off they go one by one
you won't see them until next time they come.

Paul Johnston (11)
Magherafelt High School

BABIES

Babies are great fun,
They get spoiled by their mum,
All of them love attention,
They love milk in their tum.

When babies get older,
They suck their thumb,
They look so, so comical,
Especially in bed!

Babies cry sometimes!
But not a lot,
We all love babies,
Cos they're great, great, great!

Natasha Kenning (12)
Magherafelt High School

DRUGS

Drugs can be tempting
They say they are fun,
But the harm they do
Can hurt everyone.

Think of your parents
And how they would feel
To see you die
Of ecstasy.

Drugs cost a lot of money
And how do you pay for them?
Sometimes people have to steal
In order to own them.

So if someone forces them upon you
Just ignore them,
It's not worth it
Always say no!

Karen Evans (11)
Magherafelt High School

A WITCH

A witch is black.
She is an autumn season.
She stays in a dungeon.
She is a dull, dark day.
A witch wears a long, black cloak.
A large cauldron.
She is a Hallowe'en advert: Sabrina.
A rotten potion.

Donna Young (12)
Magherafelt High School

WEATHER

It was a cold winter's day
And the wind was whistling
In the tree tops.
The snowflakes fell and made everything white
And the sky was blue and bright.
The children made snowballs
And big fat snowmen
Some men were gathering
Sticks for the fire.
Darkness fell and children
Went inside to a nice
Warm cosy house.

Matthew Bruce (11)
Magherafelt High School

MY POEM

A poem is nice
to think that it
is so much fun.
In my mind I try
to think of
a poem I like
so it
is easy if
you think hard enough.
Some of my friends say
that it is no fun
but in my mind
it is
fun for me

Stephen Scott (12)
Magherafelt High School

BASEBALL

The bowler powers up,
We all hope he's not out,
Because that's what it's all about,
Bang!
It's out of here!
Home run!
And the crowd goes wild,
You would think it was a large child,
At least the weather is mild.
Here comes the next player,
He's a bit of a sprayer
And the bowler powers up again!
Strike one!
Strike two!
Strike three!
You're out!

Ian Fentie (13)
Magherafelt High School

AUTUMN

School beckons once again.
The summer has gone,
The winds blow and there is a hint of rain.
Pupils stand by the roadside seeming alone.
The bus approaches and they disappear.
Evening comes, there is a chill in the air.
The sun glows low in the sky,
Leaves rustle underfoot,
Gold, brown and red.
They herald autumn and speak of cold, dark days to come.
Summer is a distant memory.

Steven McKee (13)
Magherafelt High School

AN AMERICAN DISASTER

What happened not so long ago,
Was terrible and horrible you know,
How people were to go on planes,
And never to come back again.

How they must have felt,
The way they checked their belts,
Holding hands and saying goodbye,
Knowing that they were going to die.

The Statue of Liberty standing proud,
Amongst the dirt and the dusty clouds,
The Twin Towers had tumbled to the ground,
And the news spread all around.

People phoning the ones they loved,
Worrying if they would go to the place above,
Americans were trying to deal with this,
Hoping and praying they would pay for this.

Stephanie Pickering (14)
Magherafelt High School

TRACTORS

Ford is the best,
You wouldn't drive the rest,
I'll put my order in for a 7610
If I get my driving test by then.

It drives along
In tune, like a melody song,
I'm sitting up so high,
I feel I could almost take off and fly.

Gazing gladly over the field
I'm thinking carefully of a good deal
And I think I'm going to have to try
To save real hard, if I want to buy.

Adam Davis (12)
Magherafelt High School

HOCUS POCUS

Hocus Pocus
Toil and trouble.
Make this cauldron
Boil and bubble.
Get me two of those
Old eyes, and two of
Those bacon pies.

Hocus Pocus
Toil and trouble.
Make this cauldron
Boil and bubble.
Get me three of
Those frog legs
And turn those children
Into clegs.

Hocus Pocus
Toil and trouble.
Make this cauldron
Boil and bubble.
Get me four of those
Children, and put them
In my boiling cauldron.

Andrea Watters (12)
Magherafelt High School

HAPPINESS

Happiness is a bright peaceful colour
like a sky blue.

It tastes like sugar and sweets
all in one.

Happiness smells like warm
melted chocolate.

It looks like a meadow
full of colour and smelly flowers.

It sounds like a flock of birds
singing joyfully to themselves
without a care in the world.

Happiness feels like soft petals
from a flower.

Robin Patton (12)
Magherafelt High School

A POEM ABOUT ENGLISH

English is a cool class,
One of those I'd like to pass.
Writing, reading, projects too,
Lots of different things we do.

If you like plays you'll have a good time,
Running about, learning your lines.
Drama groups are the best,
They will put your English to the test.

Dressing up and having fun,
Just one period there's lots to be done.
Our English teacher is totally mad,
So work hard at English and you'll be glad.

Laura Lennox (14)
Magherafelt High School

THE SEASIDE

Summer is so cool,
Summer is so fun,
Going to the seaside,
And playing in the sun.

Playing with a beach ball,
Digging with a spade,
Making castles with beach buckets,
And drinking lemonade.

'Crashing', Banging' into the waves,
Surfing into the sea,
Playing with the jellyfish,
Whilst the waves are chasing me.

Eating at the barbecue,
Sitting on the rocks,
Fiddling with the sand in our toes,
Whilst putting on our socks.

Going home is very sad,
Missing all the fun,
But I can come back another day,
To get some more of the sun.

Charlene Moore (13)
Magherafelt High School

TERRORISM

People of New York having a normal day
The planes in the sky not out to play
The suiciders in the plane were crazy people
And America's price to pay will be lethal

The plane hit the tower, boom!
This did seal the people's doom!
Thousands did the terrorists kill
Which gave them lots of evil thrill

Terrorists hear the justice warning
You won't die of global warming
You will laugh and maybe sing
But now you'll see what justice will bring.

James Redfern (13)
Magherafelt High School

PETS

I have a little dog
Jessie is her name
And every time I scold her
She thinks it is a game
I told her not to touch things
But she takes them just the same
She takes my mum's slippers
And I often get the blame!

We have six fluffy cats
They sleep out in the shed
But when they go to touch Jessie's food
They nearly lose their heads!

Caroline Hamilton (12)
Magherafelt High School

DAY AND NIGHT

Once when it was night
My really good friend got a fright
We had a good look at a star
And we thought it was really far
We also thought the same of the shiny moon
And we said the sun will come out real soon.

When out came the golden sun
I said, 'We'll have super fun.'
And I looked at the sky and watch it floating by
This thing isn't loud
But surely remember it's only a cloud.

When there's rain
People go insane.

Matthew Hagan (11)
Magherafelt High School

WHAT I'LL DREAM TONIGHT

When I go to bed at night
I lie and wonder
What I'll dream about tonight

There are nights I go to bed
And think of demons and evil
And wake up and think, 'What a nightmare!'

There are nights I go to bed
And think of peace
And wake up and think
It was the best night's sleep I ever had.

Keith McClean (13)
Magherafelt High School

SCHOOL

Teachers here, teachers there,
Rules here, rules there,
Boring work in our books,
Classes and dinners,
The dinners are like rocks.

But worst of all
There's detention, suspension and exposition.
You can hang with mates
And mess with other pupils.

But you have to work really hard
It may still be boring
But you may work!

Luigi Lupari (14)
Magherafelt High School

FIREWORKS

Fireworks, fireworks
Oh so bright
What a sight
In the night!
Flashes of colour
Red, blue and green
They're the most beautiful colours
I've ever seen.

Oh what a bang
Oh what a fright
Oh what light
All through the night.

Ryan Hepburn (13)
Magherafelt High School

EASTER

Easter is when the bunnies come out,
And when they come out we all sing and shout,
Eggs here, eggs there,
They all disappear into the air.

Chicks here, chicks there,
Laying eggs everywhere,
Chocolate, cream and boiled eggs too,
They are all made for you.

Rolling and hiding eggs,
Is fun to do,
But eating too many eggs,
Is hard luck for you.

When Easter goes we hope and say,
'Please Mr Bunny, can you not stay?'

Wendy Evans (13)
Magherafelt High School

THE MOON

I am the moon
I sleep all day and shine all night,
I glow all night as bright as a night-light,
I sit and talk to the man on the moon
Who laughs as hard as me the moon.
I love to watch all the people sleep,
Then try not to let them see me peep.
I also love to shine with all my might,
Until I say . . . goodnight

Laura McKeown (11)
Magherafelt High School

HOME RULES

Get up for school!
Get changed!
Get your breakfast
Brush your teeth!
Make the bed!
Get your bag!
Off you go!
Bell rings . . .
We all go home.
Get changed!
Hoover your room!
Go out and play!
Come in for dinner!
Go and play!
Come in for supper!
Brush your teeth and go to bed
You have school in the morning!

Christina Heaney (12)
Magherafelt High School

FRIENDS!

F   unny
R   eliable
I   rresistible
E   njoyable
N   ice
D   esirable
S   ociable

Laura Downey (12)
Magherafelt High School

TEARS FROM AMERICA!

On just a normal Tuesday morning
Disaster struck on the famous World Trade Towers.
Two planes crashed with a very big bang.
People thought it was an accident
But they were so very wrong.

Two planes were hijacked
And evil, cruel, heartless men
Killed thousands of people.
There were tears and broken hearts
Throughout the world.

Families and friends shocked
And waiting to hear if their loved ones are dead.

This tragic day will go down in history
And people who did this
Will be brought to justice.

God bless the families.

Sarah Hyndman (14)
Magherafelt High School

MONSTER TRUCKS!

Monster trucks . . . like giants standing proud and tall
Like mighty monsters with dare devil drivers.
They will crash, smash and bash anyone or anything in the way!
The engines roaring with power and with such speed.
The competitions are starting - it's a show of strength,
Who will be the best?

James Porter (13)
Magherafelt High School

EMOTION POEM

Happiness is the colour of blue
Happiness tastes like blue ice cream
Happiness smells like a pink rose
Happiness looks like bright colours
Happiness sounds like nice music
Happiness feels like love of your family

John Smyth (12)
Magherafelt High School

FEAR

Fear is black.
It tastes like blood pudding
And smells like burning wood.
Fear looks like a ball of flames.
It sounds like banging on the wall.
Fear is life threatening!

Trevor Gibson (12)
Magherafelt High School

MY HEART

I wish I had looked after my heart,
And not have eaten the tart.
For folk might say you'll be on the cart,
All because you ate that tart.

Oh I wish I'd looked after my heart,
Because I'm falling apart.
The calories I fear will be high on the chart,
Oh I wish I had looked after my heart.

So now I'll look after my heart,
Be wise and go by my chart.
Exercise, diet will all play a part,
At last I'll look after my heart.

Helen Hutchinson (11)
Magherafelt High School

GOLF!

Golf, a sport for gentlemen
With clubs of high standards.
And golf balls of all sorts
Nike, Dunlop, Slazenger and Wilson.
With memberships of £100 or £200
For Moyola and Portrush (The Royal).

Hole one, 365 yards from the tee-off,
To the green, and the hole.
Concentrating on the ball with a three wood.
The take back slow, but still concentrating.
It's fast on the swing and what a shot!
Half way up the fairway.
Next a five iron and *smack!*
The ball's on the green.
The last move *the putt.*

The *putt*, the worst part of the game.
I wonder what Tiger Woods would do?
I bet he would line the ball up with the hole.
So that's what I'll do.
I have the ball in line and it's in the hole.
One under par!

John Montgomery (13)
Magherafelt High School

CHRISTMAS

Christmas Eve has finally come
Eveyrone is excited
Hurry up, get into bed
Before he leaves the presents.

Christmas morn has now come
Running down the stairs
Standing in the living room
With lots and lots of presents.

We unwrap them all
And play with them for hours
Barbies, Action Men and teddy bears
All for us today.

Christmas dinner
Oh! So hungry
Hummy, hummy, hummy
Ice cakes, celebrations and all the lovely sweets.

Now it's come to the end of the day
So tired, but excited
From all we've done today!

Kyla Bowman (11)
Magherafelt High School

STARLIGHT

The moon shines bright
In the night
Like a silver coin
In the light

The sky looks like fiery flames
As the stars in the sky
Look like they're fighting
In the night.

Moon and stars
Fiery flames
These things are all part of
Starlight.

Leanne Sands (11)
Magherafelt High School

BUSH DECLARES WAR

One day in New York
A disaster happened
The World Trade Centre blew up
The cause of the accident was two
Planes that were hijacked by Afghanistan men
President Bush thought it through for a while
He decides on an action
Bush declares war.

The American troops know that they have
British troops on their side
With Pakistan and Uzberistan letting troops through
Afghanistan can't escape
With air, land and sea
Bush begins war.

In the end we know who will win
Because Bush and the British
Won't let America down
In the end the country that will cheer
Will be stripes and the stars
In the end the good flag will fly high
The good red, white and blue
Bush will win the war.

Alastair Bigger (14)
Magherafelt High School

HALLOWE'EN NIGHT

On Hallowe'en night I went out to play,
But wondered what my parents would say,
I was dressed as a witch,
Oh what a fitch.

My friends met me at my front door,
I could not believe Sally was dressed as a boar,
We went trick or treating down the town,
And Betty had such an ugly frown.

We went to my friend's cool house,
And watched her cat chase my pet mouse,
The fireworks were really so loud,
When her mother walked in she bowed.

The clock at twelve did strike,
And I gave a loud, *'Yike!'*
The lights were flickering and flashing,
And the electric was bashing.

It was really so scary
'I am so scared,' said Gerry,
We ran up to our own houses,
When I was running I heard all of these funny noises.

I got to my front door and rang the bell,
No one answered so I gave a loud yell,
Mum then had answered so I got in,
And while I was in I was holding my shin.

My mum watched as I was in terror,
And saw me pull my brown silky hair,
Suddenly the electric went off,
And I gave big cough.

We then went to bed to have a good sleep,
And while I was in bed I gave a good peep.

Tracy Seffen (11)
Magherafelt High School

WORLD TRADE CENTRE

Two towers stood still alongside
So strong, so straight, so tall
Specially designed to never fall
The Americans were so proud of them all.

Then one day in September 2001
The day had only just begun
At twenty to nine all was fine!
Two planes had lifted from their airports, according to time.
But a short time later they crashed into the Towers
And part of New York was like a coal mine.

The dust and rubble came tumbling down.
Some of those poor people would never be found!
The World Trade Centre was now all on the ground
While people panicked all around!

The heartache and fears,
The moans and tears
Friends and colleagues, loved so dear
Were wiped away
On that September day.

Gemma Davis (13)
Magherafelt High School

STARTING SCHOOL

Getting ready for school to start,
Sorting out pens, pencils, rulers and files,
Going up the town to buy my uniform,
And to choose my school bag and shoes.

Tomorrow's the day - all excited, can't sleep!
Have to get up at 7.30,
Packed my bag all set to go,
Stomach sore - because I'm nervous.

Meeting new friends and all the teachers,
Trying to find my way round the school,
All the older pupils yawning and dreading,
To go to their next class.

Home time - yippee!
Can't wait until the day's out,
'Cause I am looking forward,
To going back to school the very next day.

Rebecca Scott (11)
Magherafelt High School

AUTUMN

Oh how I love the autumn time
The crisp clear air and bright sunshine
Glinting through trees of reds, yellows and golds
Such a beautiful scene for one to behold.

The harvest time reaps to an end once again
As the combine rolls through the barley and corn
The pheasants strut along the hedges and fields
Searching for grains to have as a meal.

The apples, plums and blackberries too
Have all been picked except for a few
Berries of red to attract the birds
My favourite season which is the third.

And in the early morning light
Gleams misty grass and cobwebs white
It paints a picture of harmony and peace
But sadly it's only a short term lease.

Craig Ritchie (11)
Magherafelt High School

FIREWORKS

Fireworks are spectacular
So many colours
So many sounds.

There are cartwheels,
Which go whizzing around
In bright colours
Which fall to the ground.

Rockets soar into the sky
Bursting in colours
Reds, greens, purples
Silver and golds
Then fade and die.

Children with sparklers
Their arms outstretched
Holding tight as the sparklers crackle
And their faces turn bright
I remember it all
On that Hallowe'en night.

Lynsey Brown (11)
Magherafelt High School

DISASTER

Just a normal day
The busiest time of all
When disaster struck
Making New York's ground tremble
And sky fill with smoke
A jet flying oh so low
Hit one of the twin towers
As it if wasn't bad enough
Twenty minutes later
Another tower was hit
More noise, more smoke
People screaming
Mass panic as people flee
Others jumping to their deaths
Now New York was in chaos
At 10.05 the south tower collapses
Smoke, dust and carnage
People running to safety
Others dying in the flames
Then at 10.28 the north tower collapses
People confused
People hoping
People mourning
People lost
People found
What will we do?

Kelly Hamilton (14)
Magherafelt High School

SOUNDS AT SCHOOL

Bell ringing
Pupils yawning
Lessons beginning
A few find it boring
Bell ringing
Pupils eating
Some laughing
Chairs screeching
Teachers nagging
Peoples' feet racing
Till closing
Pupils talking
Bell ringing
Classes starting
People rushing
Some dashing
Very few waiting
Lessons boring
Bell ringing
People cheering
Chairs screeching
Teachers nagging
Some whining
Bell ringing
Pupils shouting
Home time!

Jennifer Brown (11)
Magherafelt High School

SCHOOL

We go to school five days a week
To get an education
We meet with friends
And have a chat
But then that hateful bell rings - *drat!*

We go to school five days a week
To get an education
We learn French and science
And English too
With teachers watching over everything we do.

We go to school five days a week
To get an education
We sit all day with pen in hand
Writing *far* too much
That all just seems like double Dutch.

If only we could stay at home five days a week
And lie in bed all day
Eat and sleep and watch TV
And do no work at all
But instead of teachers
We'd have to listen to our parents nag and call.

Roberta Bolton (14)
Magherafelt High School

CUBE

I am a cube not a tube
With six faces I'm bound to be a cube
I've got a friend that can bend
And if I'm broken I'm hard to mend

Mark Stewart (12)
Magherafelt High School

INSIDE MY HEAD

There are tractors
and motorbikes
and huge, fast racing cars
and an exciting game of football

There is my grandpa's farm
and my uncle's calves
for me to feed
There is swimming
and playing on my go-cart

I think of my uncle's car
for me to drive
I think of Bonzo
with a great big bone
and I think of
my granny and the bread van
with all those delicious sweets
and I am happy.

Andrew McKinley (13)
Magherafelt High School

SCHOOL

S   is for sleepy when I get up
C   is for crazy for school to end
H   is for hard, the work is very
O   is for oh I forgot to do my homework!
O   is for oh I forgot to bring my books!
L   is for lessons long and boring.

Alison Campbell (13)
Magherafelt High School

I Want a Pet

A cuddly cat, oh maybe not,
A little puppy, call him Lucky,
Hammy the hamster,
Now he could be handful.

I want a pet
What about a tiny mouse?
'Oh no,' my mother shouts,
'It won't be coming in this house!'

A lop-eared bunny,
Now that could be funny,
A big fat rat,
He'd better not eat Mum's mats.

Do I really want a pet?
Oh no perhaps maybe not.

Vicky Cross (11)
Magherafelt High School

High School

'H urry up or you'll be late.'
'I 'll be down in a minute.'
'G ood.'
'H urry up, there's your bus away down past.'

S econds later sitting in school
'C ome on, or we'll be late for class.'
'H old on, wait for me.'
'O h, that was my foot.'
'O h, and that was my head.'
L ong last back at home, home sweet home.

Shirley-Anne York (11)
Magherafelt High School

AUTUMN

Autumn is my favourite time of the year,
With the leaves falling everywhere.
The nights are not as clear,
And it gets dark very early around here.

The leaves turn brown,
Softly falling to the ground.
Crunchy and soft they are everywhere,
And the trees are left bare.

The only thing I don't like about autumn very much
Is the fact
We can't get out to play
Because it's a shorter day.

Christmas time is drawing near,
To end yet another year.
With Christmas lights,
To brighten up our dark nights.

Yet once again autumn has slipped by,
For yet another year,
And soon the buds will reappear,
And spring will start another year.

Vicki Porter (12)
Magherafelt High School

RUGBY

R   is for rough
U   is for ugly
G   is for good fun
B   is for blood
Y   is for youths

Ryan Logan (13)
Magherafelt High School

GEORGE

My pony George,
He died in August.
His nickname's Teddy.
His soft brown fur
I cuddle up to.
His friend Lady
Missing him so
She needs a new friend
George is a Shetland
With a white blaze
And a black spot on his bum
He always bucked me off
Little devil
He lived to almost 40!
That is a big age
You just swing your leg high
And you are on him
It's awful in the summer
He's got so much fur
He's like a big ball
Of brown wool.

G   inger George
E   ars big and furry brown
O   ver the poles
R   ound the jumps the Shetland goes
G   alloping across the fields
E   agerly jumping over jumps

Cordelia Mulholland (11)
Magherafelt High School

CHRISTMAS

At Christmas time,
The fairy lights shine,
Santa will soon be here,
As Christmas day is drawing near.

The presents are wrapped neatly under the tree,
The children are laughing and shouting with glee,
The decorations are hanging brightly,
We watch as the first snowflakes are falling lightly.

The children are playing in the snow,
Then come inside to sit at the fire's warm glow,
The Christmas pudding is cooking slowly,
As we remember Jesus Christ born in a stable so lowly.

Christmas morning is here at last,
The snowflakes are now falling fast,
The children run quickly down the stairs,
To see what Santa has left to be theirs.

Under the tree sits presents galore,
Wrapping paper soon covers the floor,
We sing Christmas carols by the fire,
I don't think we'll ever tire.

Now the New Year is arriving,
People are sending good wishes and glad tidings,
In hope of a joyful year all round,
Until once again Christmas time is bound.

Elaine McGeagh (13)
Magherafelt High School

HER

She is gone now, she is dead,
I think about her in my bed.
I dream about her every night,
And then again in morning light.

Why did she have to go?
I guess I will never know.
Maybe it was just meant to be,
Although that is something I cannot see.

This thing I hold so deep inside,
This eternal hurting, I just ask why?
Why a little girl so sweet,
I hope I'm destined again to meet.

I hope she's happy, way up there,
With the man who's in my prayers.
Laughing, playing, I don't care,
If she's with the man upstairs.

Nigel Kells (13)
Magherafelt High School

HAPPINESS

Happiness is bright red
It tastes like raspberry ice cream
Happiness is the smell in spring like a new blossomed flower
It sounds like Christmas carols
It looks like United supporters when they score a goal
It feels like a warm summer's day
And you're in an outdoor pool with a ice-cold drink.

David Brooks (13)
Magherafelt High School

SUMMER

Summer is a time of sun,
When there is lots of fun,
Sometimes we go to the beach,
Where we make sand castles and play in the water.

Summer is a time of sun,
When there is lots of fun,
We usually go on holiday,
When we can relax and meet new friends.

Summer is a time of sun,
When there is lots of fun,
We don't have to go to school,
So we have more time for things we want to do.

Summer is a time of sun,
When there is lots of fun,
We can go for a walk in the countryside,
And view the beautiful sights.

Stewart Miller (12)
Magherafelt High School

SCIENCE

S   cience is an exciting subject
C   hemicals mixing together
I   nformation buzzing round your head
E   xperimenting . . . I wish it could last forever
N   othing is better than discovering something new
C   hemistry is a type of science
E   verything to do with science is always interesting

Elaine Gilmour (11)
Magherafelt High School

TREASURE HUNT

Round the trees and up the hill,
Like a pack of wolves -
Down the hill and past the church,
Let's *hope* we don't see anything.
I've walked a *mile,* this map is useless,
Oh wait, an arrow of rocks!

Turning left and turning right, under and over,
Will this ever end!
School! I've been walking around in circles, just my luck.
Everyone is going left,
Hurry, let's catch them.

I've turned right, where is everyone else?
Oh wait, another clue!
A piece of paper saying,
'Walk a mile, turn left at Old Road
Maybe you'll be lucky.'
I could be right.

I've done what I've been told to do, what a surprise,
I'm walking towards the village shop
Waiting to see another clue
But instead I find what I'm looking for
My prize is . . .
A big fat tick for doing sooo well!

Lauren Lennox (12)
Magherafelt High School

A DAY IN SEPTEMBER

The terrorists take over the planes.
Threatening the passengers with pain.
They change the destination.
Telling the people to be patient.
The first plane starts to soar into
The first Trade Centre.
This was a day in September.

They think it is an accident.
People are worried and run
Trying to save their lives.
They race out of the buildings
But the pace was too slow.
Another plane crashes into the
Second Trade Centre.
This was a day in September.

The whole world is in shock
But the worst is yet to come.
All of a sudden both trade centres crumble.
Thousands are missing, possibly dead
Emergency services are on that same street.
Americans say, 'This is not the end!
This is the beginning of war!'

Allan Keatley (13)
Magherafelt High School